The Trekking Guide
ชีวิตข้าไกด์ทัวร์ป่า

Yao Sripuri

Copyright © Punsawat Sripuri, 2024

All rights reserved. This book or any portion thereof may not be reproduced or used in any manner whatsoever without the express written permission of the publisher.

yao1000smiles@yahoo.com

ISBN: 9798300177560

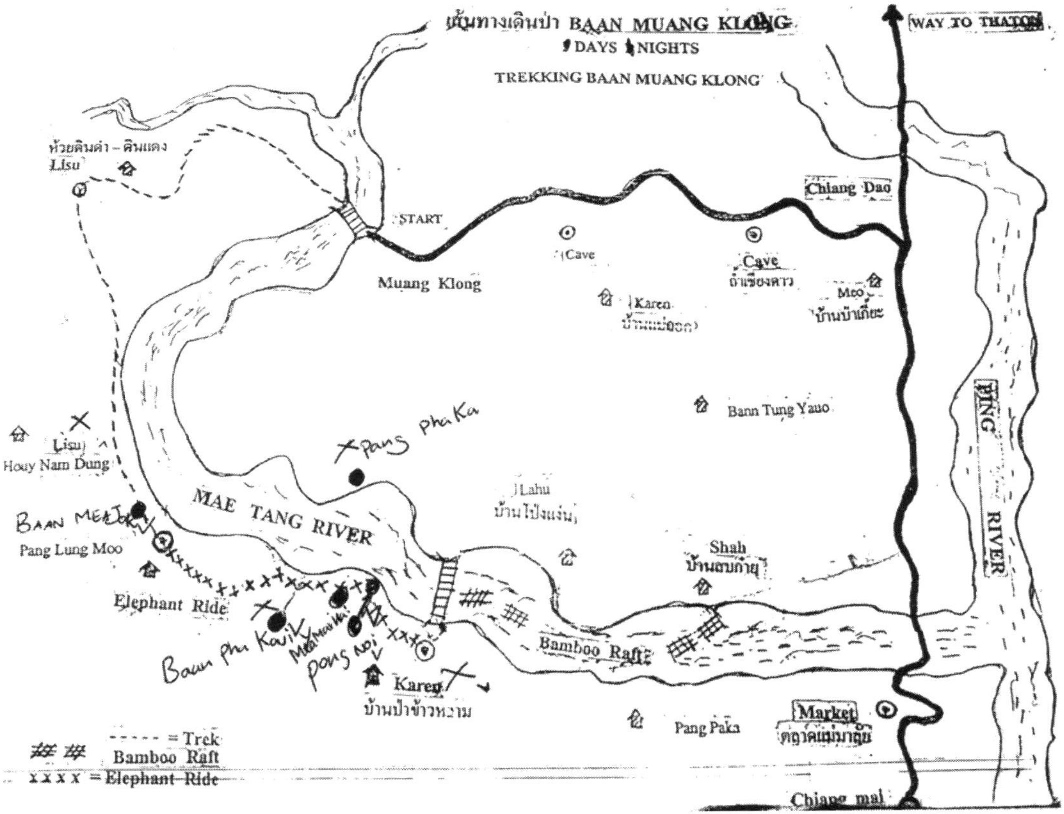
เส้นทางเดินป่า BAAN MUANG KLONG
DAYS NIGHTS
TREKKING BAAN MUANG KLONG
WAY TO THATON
Lisu
START
Muang Klong
Cave
Cave
Karen
Chiang Dao
Meo
Bann Tung Yauo
pang phaKa
Lisu
Houy Nam Dung
MAE TANG RIVER
Lahu
BAAN MEATORY
Pang Lung Moo
Shah
PING RIVER
Elephant Ride
Baan pha Kovik
pong noi
Karen
Bamboo Raft
Pang Paka
Market
Chiang mai
- - - - = Trek
Bamboo Raft
x x x x = Elephant Ride

Contents

Chapter 1 - Life is an Adventure 1

Chapter 2 - Life is a Journey 5

Chapter 3 - Life is a Challenge 9

Chapter 4 - Life is a Destiny 14

Chapter 5 - Life is a Pleasure 20

Chapter 6 - The Trekking Guide 24

Chapter 7 - Life is Blowing in the Wind 30

Chapter 8 - Life is Fun 38

Chapter 9 - Life is Always Changing 44

Chapter 10 - Life Must Go On 48

Chapter 11 - Life is Like a River 58

Chapter 12 - Life is an Illusion 65

Chapter 13 - Life is Letting Go 72

Chapter 14 - Life is Beautiful 87

Chapter 15 - Life is a Nature Lesson 101

Introduction

The Lord Buddha said that it is extremely difficult to be born as a human being. It's like a blind turtle that lives in the middle of a great ocean. Imagine a hoop the size of the turtle's head floating on the water. If, on one day every hundred years, the turtle surfaces and happens to put its head through the hoop, that's how difficult it is.

In honour of my father and mother, I want to record and remember the little things that have happened in my life. Through characters such as close relatives, friends and people that I have had the good fortune to meet, there are many stories that I would like to record as a souvenir for future generations.

I must first say that I am not a professional writer, but someone who likes to write and read a little. If there are any errors in this book I would like to offer my apologies.

I wrote this book with some inspiration in my heart, wanting to tell you all, the readers, about my simple background. It's the story of the life of a poor country boy who struggled to achieve a better life. I sincerely hope that the stories I present in this book will provide some ideas and inspiration for you in your own lives.

I have tried to incorporate some of the principles and teachings of the Lord Buddha as guidance for living together in this world with happiness and peace and in harmony with nature.

The Trekking Guide is a book that directly relates to my own life and my career as a trekking guide. The aim is to share my experiences and the fun and memories of the past decades.

I apologize to any friends whose names I have mentioned without asking their permission first. There is no intention to mock or belittle anyone.

Jungle tours are one of the top attractions in Thailand. I believe they are a way of creating new experiences for tourists and also bringing income into the country. In particular they improve education opportunities for poorer people in the countryside who get the chance to practice speaking foreign languages with tourists when they go to spend time in the villages.

At the same time they reveal to the world the natural beauty of the jungle and the way of life and culture of the hilltribes who live in the high mountains in the northern region of Thailand.

Trekking tours have become a popular trend for tourists who like to experience nature and adventure in the mountains with local tour guides. They are together for a short period of time - 3 days, 2 nights or more - on a journey up and down hills, across rivers and through the forest. They travel on foot, by elephant and on bamboo rafts and stay overnight in remote villages in a totally different environment to the city, experiencing the simple way of life of the hilltribe people.

The special thing about jungle tours is that everyone learns to share, help and care for each other during activities and this has led to stories of love and compassion between people who have different religions, languages and cultures. These interactions occur between foreign tourists and trekking guides, porters, mahouts, raft operators and even among tourists themselves. Indeed, an American magazine once listed jungle tours in Chiang Mai among the top ten places in the world to find a boyfriend or girlfriend.

I hope this book brings you enjoyment and enhances your knowledge of Thailand. If you are a trekking guide or a tourist who has been on a trek, it might bring a smile to your face when you remember past adventures.

I dedicate this book to my father and mother, who raised and nurtured me as well as to all dear friends both named and unnamed.

Wishing happiness and well-being to all of you readers, your encouragement is the nectar that feeds my soul.

With love and respect
Yao Sripuri ('Jungle Boy')

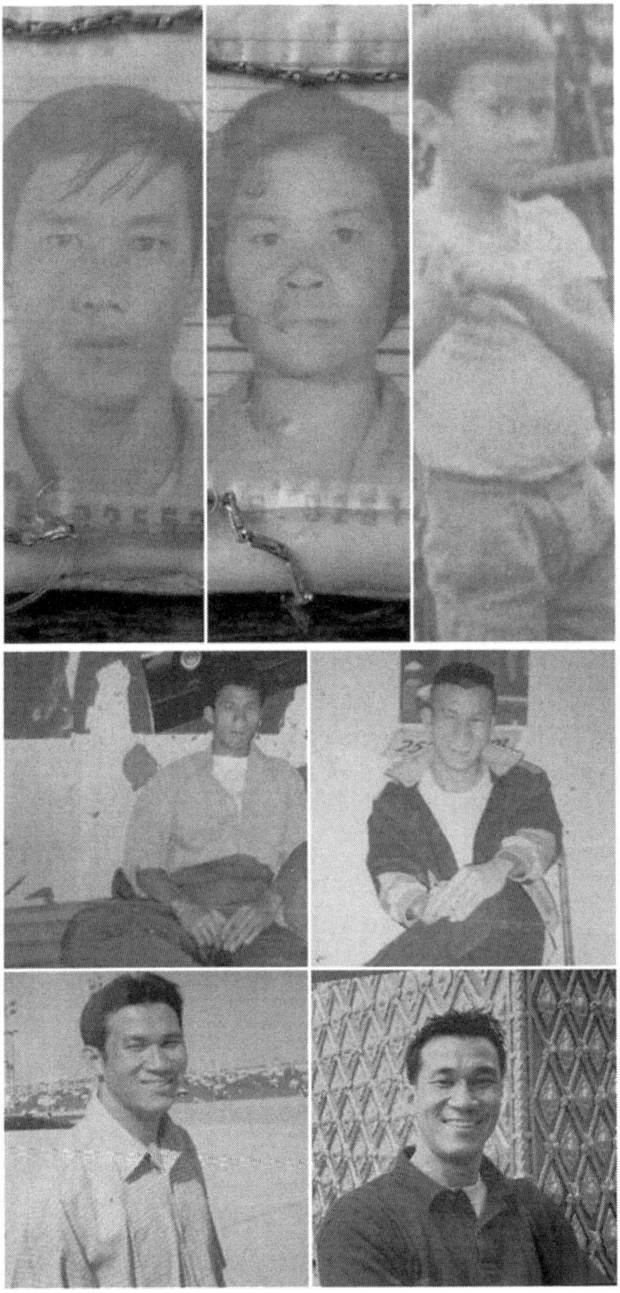

Chapter 1 - Life is an Adventure

I was born in a small village in Chiang Rai province in 1970. I remember that in those days it wasn't very developed. The roads were still dirt roads and very bumpy. During the dry season, they were dusty and when the rainy season arrived they were wet and muddy. Electricity had not yet reached all areas. My village was not too far from the city, about twenty kilometres, but in those days it seemed far away from the civilization of the city of Chiang Rai.

I heard from my mother that Mother Su, a village elder, was the midwife who delivered me in my parents' small hut. The village where I was born was called San Nong Bua, with no more than twenty households. It was a branch of the main village, Ban Mae Khao Tom Tha Sut. There was a small lake with an abundance of shrimp, crab and fish and lots of wild edible plants and crops around it. It was like a giant natural larder that sustained the people. Whoever needed to could go there to gather food for their family.

I have therefore had a strong connection with nature and have loved the forest life since childhood. When I was a kid, I liked to run around with my friends in that village. It was a simple way of life because each family had the same farming background. Life in those days, fifty years ago, was simple but full of warmth between villagers who lived together with kindness and generosity.

Most of the population of Thailand is Buddhist, and in those days they still strictly followed the teachings of Buddha. For people in the countryside, the temple was the place where everyone gathered to make merit according to traditions and various customs inherited from their ancestors. It was also a place for entertainment – whenever there was an event such as a ceremony or a festival, it took place at the temple. It was where people went to relax and socialise.

I walked almost three kilometres to and from school every day with my friends. Every time I think about my past and my childhood, it fills me with happiness because it was an innocent and simple life. The village was rich in natural resources with forests, streams full of fish and rice paddies providing food. Although there were no facilities like today, the villagers seemed happy. I could see the joy in their eyes.

Unfortunately, this simple way of life, close to nature has almost completely disappeared from rural Thailand now. Although there are more modern conveniences than before, these things have damaged and changed the simple way of life. Today, people are in a rush and looking for personal gain unlike in the past when people lived modestly, supported each other and had more respect for nature.

I was born into a poor family of five siblings. I am the fourth child with three brothers and one sister. My mother, the youngest child of my grandfather and grandmother, was born in Phan District, Chiang Rai province. She later moved to Mae Khao Tom Tha Sut village.

She told me how she met my father. One day she was herding buffaloes with her friends of the same age, far away from her village, when she was gored in the chest and passed out. By chance my father was also taking care of buffaloes in that area. He helped my mother and was able to take her safely to her parents' house on the back of a buffalo. Thanks to his kind actions, my grandparents decided that my father was a good man and they arranged for my mother to live with him after that.

My father was a heavy drinker and was nicknamed the village drunk. When I was a child, I was often teased by my friends because of this. I was very embarrassed and not understanding the situation, I was often angry with my father. However, he was a good person. Even though he didn't study and he couldn't read or write, he worked hard to raise and support us.

My mother, who has always been a hero in my eyes, didn't learn to read and write either, but her teachings were simple and valuable in my life. In those days, you had to obey your parents and you weren't allowed to answer back, but I always did. Even so, I never received harsh punishments from my parents and they made sure we all received a basic education.

During my childhood, I had to help my mother with almost everything she asked even though I was lazy and wanted to play with my friends. Because I was born into poor family, I had to help my parents with all the jobs that they asked me to do. When I think about my childhood I'm proud I was born into this family. Poverty taught me to be strong and able to fight things very well.

My last year of compulsory education was at the end of primary school. I wanted to continue my studies, but I couldn't because of our financial situation. The only way for children from poor families to continue their studies in those days was to be ordained as a novice monk and study in a temple.

I had to leave home at the age of twelve to be a temple boy and learn to take care of myself. In 1984 I was ordained as a novice at Nang Lae temple along with other boys of my age from Nang Lae and Ban Du subdistricts. I have lived apart from my parents ever since.

During that time, I had the opportunity to learn many things from Phra Ajarn (teachers) who were monks who had studied at temples in Bangkok. The training period of just one month made a little boy like me eager to continue learning. After the programme ended, everyone returned to their home temples. Some boys whose parents could afford it went to study at secondary school, but I had to seek knowledge within the temple walls.

Life within the temple had many rules and regulations based on the teachings of the Lord Buddha that monks had to learn and follow. The daily routine required waking up at 5 am to say prayers in a group with novices, seniors and the next generation of temple children. It was a valuable experience for me. Even so, we were still kids and when the head monk wasn't looking we found a way to play football and do boxing and other things that kids do.

Every morning we went out to collect alms (meals from the people in the village) just like birds flying out of the nest in search of food. We were assigned duties every day and learned how to help with tidying, cleaning and sweeping the temple courtyard.

The most important thing however was to study various prayers in order to preserve the traditions of the Buddhist way of life so that we could pass them on to the next generations. Something that helped form my views on life and humanity was reading Handbook for Mankind and some thoughts of the master monk named Buddhadasa Bhikkhu. The principles and teachings in the book gave me a whole new perspective and I saw the value of being born as a human being, as the Dharma teachings of the Buddha said, that life is impermanent and birth and death are a natural part of life. We need to understand that we are born to fight to survive day by day. All the things that we try to achieve during our lifetime can't be taken with us when we die and happiness and suffering are merely illusions.

All this knowledge gave me the strength to fight harder. I no longer felt humiliated or asked myself why I was such a poor man. In this life we have two choices, we can live our lives doing good or live our lives doing evil.

Life is an adventure!

Chapter 2 - Life is a Journey

All life that is born on this earth is here for a different reason. Nobody can choose when they are born, but everybody is born with a dream, to want to do something, to follow their heart's desire. Every person has different goals, but we are all given one brain and two hands.

What way of life were you born into? A poor family, or the family of a billionaire? If by chance you were born into a rich family, where food is always available, you can travel wherever you want and you are able to easily achieve your dreams, your life is probably not that difficult. But if you happened to be born into a family which some days has almost nothing to eat, life will be challenging.

The path is sometimes very clear, but there is no right way to walk it. There are many obstacles, rules and regulations of a complicated society. But still, if you are a fighter, strong-willed, dare to face any obstacles big or small and are not afraid of failure, you have the chance to achieve your dreams. This life is yours - make it worthwhile.

At the age of twelve I finished the summer novice ordination programme and began studying the Dharma (the teachings of the Lord Buddha) at the temple in my village. I studied there together with my friends from the neighbouring village for three years.

Then I had the opportunity to do a correspondence course in general education until the end of high school. I still lived at the temple and once a week I went to Chiang Rai to meet the teachers and other students. When I completed the course I was 16 years old and confused about life at that time. What should I do next?

My friends went to study in other places to pursue their dreams. My close friends Somsong Wongkaew and Chan Phankaew went to study at Wat Phra Kaew temple in Chiang Rai. I often visited them there and it allowed me to get to know many other friends such as Wichai Kawichai, Chaiya Khammuang and Krit Laemchad, who are still close friends to this day.

I still didn't know what I wanted to do. What was next? If I stayed in my hometown, my life would stay the same. Other novice monks like me left to pursue a career in farming because that's what their parents wanted.

One day I had the opportunity to go to the Chiang Saen district to visit the Golden Triangle where Thailand, Myanmar and Laos all meet at the Mekong River. There were many tourists. Thai people and foreigners came to visit this area every day because of the unique cool climate and very beautiful nature. As I walked around, I saw a man standing and talking to about twenty foreigners who were all captivated by his words. I stood there in amazement and thought to myself "Amazing! How can you talk to these golden-haired foreigners so easily?". I imagined myself being able to speak the language of these people.

When I arrived back at my village on that day, my dreams were strongly ignited in my heart. I was inspired. I was going to do what this man could do and I began to look for places where I could learn western languages.

I started learning the English language by reading books and I asked some friends if they could find a place for me to study. Then I remembered my friend Wichai Kawichai who had travelled to study in Chiang Mai after his time at the Wat Phra Kaew temple in Chiang Rai. I will never forget this friend. He is someone who has always been there to help me and advise me on my studies.

One day I went to visit him to find a place to learn English and somewhere to live. He's such a good friend that he led me to many temples in Chiang Mai, however the abbot of each temple wanted a novice who would study the Dharma (Lord Buddha's teachings). Because my wish was to come to learn a language, I didn't meet the criteria, so I was rejected from many temples until finally I went to live in one of the temples in the Mae Rim district, Arunniwat temple. The abbot was a very kind person and allowed me to stay there.

My dream was saved by this new place. I had travelled far away from my hometown to begin living here. I knew the road ahead would be tough, but because of this opportunity I was not going to give up.

I started looking for a place to study whilst also searching for more English textbooks to read. I asked many friends if there was any place that offered language teaching. One day, I went to study at the Northern Language Centre which was one of the biggest modern institutes in Chiang Mai. I studied there for three terms, however, my family became concerned about finances since it was very expensive. It was challenging for poor countrymen like me and I had to stop studying there because there was not enough tuition money. Once again, I asked for advice from my friends on where I could learn.

A book that is very valuable to me is Standard English Grammar, written by Ajarn Samran Khamying, which I used as a guide to learn English. Every day I picked up this book, read it and scribbled in it. I still remember well every morning when I went on the alms round (collecting food for the monks), I wrote English words on the alms bowl. I can remember one person was waiting to offer food to me. I stopped and accidentally said in English, "Good morning!". They looked at me very confused!

At the temple, the abbot would receive the newspaper the Thai Rath Daily News. The first page I always read was by Mr Saengchai Sunthornwatana. He was a columnist who used to live in America and returned to Thailand to write a column for the Thai Rath newspaper about the American way of life and slang words. I read it every day and secretly saved it to memorise and practise.

Sometimes novices and monks in the same temple would think I was really crazy because I would practice conversations with the trees. One day a friend told me to visit the Wat Phra Singh temple. This is a very old temple with a beautiful pagoda and one of the most famous Buddha statues in Chiang Mai. It has a long history, so lots of foreign tourists come to visit every day. My friend recommended that I should go there to practice talking to foreign people. It was a brilliant and exciting idea, talking directly to native speakers!

Every day, I took a bus from the temple in the Mae Rim district to travel to Wat Phra Singh. I would go up to tourists and introduce myself to practice speaking the language. Many of them were kind and asked me questions about the temple. I volunteered to be a guide and I would say to tourists "Hello! How are you? Can I help you with anything?".

I practiced speaking nearly every day so I could improve my skills and self-confidence quickly. And the most important thing is that there were no tuition fees, which made it accessible to poor novices like me. Practicing with native speakers directly resulted in greater learning than attending a language school. When I mispronounced words, tourists would be very helpful and suggest tips to improve my English. At this point in my life, my target was to practice here and become proficient.

Although I was not a student of the Thammarat Suksa school (high school for monks) of Wat Phra Singh, this place is very important to me. I got to know many new friends here and I found out that most tour guides in Chiang Mai graduated from this school.

I had finally found the best way to improve my English by that point, so I bought some Japanese language books to study and practice in the same way. When I met Japanese tourists, I practiced speaking Japanese. Why did I love to study other languages? The answer is because I didn't have to pay tuition fees.

Whatever you try, you will always find success. I couldn't remember where I had heard this from, but I believed it was true. If we set our minds to doing anything with determination, success will surely come to us.

I intended to practice learning both English and Japanese almost every day. It gave me confidence that I was on the right path to success. By now I had set my target and I knew I just had to run towards that destination. I was working hard and the rest was left to God.

Life is a journey!

Chapter 3 - Life is a Challenge

To make your dream a reality you need to have determination, challenge and focus, but the most important thing is to follow your heart. Ambition is a wonderful thing that pushes us try to our best to overcome large or small obstacles in order to reach our goals. It's a serious test for everyone.

During my stay at Wat Arunniwat, I travelled to Wat Phra Singh nearly every day to improve my English. Some of my friends who were studying at high school had accommodation in this temple so I was allowed to use it as a place to relax sometimes.

One of my friends with whom I spent a lot of time lived in Chiang Mai. He was a young novice from Lampang named Somchai Jai-in. His life story was just like mine - he came from a poor family and wanted to have a better life. I met him at Wat Phra Singh while I was learning to speak with foreign tourists. He also went there to do the same thing. We have been good friends from that time until now.

We met almost every day at Wat Phra Singh and sometimes we went to other temples that tourists liked to visit. When you meet foreigners don't be shy, but make sure you choose the right target. There were foreigners who lived in Chiang Mai and they were not interested in talking to us. You could assume that if you saw someone holding a camera and a map in their hands that they might like to get some information from you.

Once I went to talk to a foreigner and when I asked him in English "Can you speak Thai?", he replied to me "Pom oo kham muang kho dai", meaning "I can speak Chiang Mai dialect" – I felt so embarrassed! Every day I enjoyed my life learning to speak English and Japanese by practicing with tourists. I sometimes went to visit my good friend Wichai Kawichai from Chiang Rai who I mentioned before. He lived in Wat Sridonchai temple near the Night Bazaar. Wichai was a very good student, his dream was to become a policeman in the future. I saw that he wrote in his notebook that he wouldn't return to his hometown if he didn't reach his goal. It made me more determined to fight for my own future.

Looking at my friends at that time, everyone was enthusiastic about studying and finding success in life. Surachat Najai, a younger novice who stayed at the same temple as Wichai, always came to talk to me, asking if he would be able to speak foreign languages. I was able to speak two languages – English and a little Japanese - and I sometimes took tourists to visit the temple where he lived. It inspired him to do the same as I was doing. I told him, "If you have a dream, a huge challenge is waiting to test you. If you are still breathing, that means you've got a chance to stand and fight for it. Everybody has one life, a brain and two hands. If you try hard and don't give up, you can do anything". He was determined to learn Japanese until he could speak it very well. Many years later, I heard that he had a successful career as a Japanese tour guide.

Another friend that I must mention is Somboon Wachirabunsuk who inspired and challenged me. Somboon and I joined the novice ordination programme at the same time. We lived in the same sub-district, but different villages. At that time, children from Nang Lae subdistrict and Ban Du subdistrict, especially children who came from poor families, enrolled in the ordination programme as novices to continue studying Lord Buddha's teachings. This was the only way that these children could get a better education. It also helped to preserve Buddha's teachings in order to sustain the Dharma.

When the programme was finished and each novice went back to the temple of their hometown, there were competitive exams to find clever novices to study in Bangkok. My friend Somboon was one of those who was chosen and in 1985 he moved to study at the marble temple (Benchamabophit) in Bangkok. After that I didn't have the opportunity to see my friend again and we lost contact for a long time.

One day, the abbot and the teacher from the Buddhist school in the temple where I lived in Chiang Mai arranged an educational tour taking students to study and travel in Bangkok. We were allowed to go inside Benchamabophit temple and stay overnight there so I was able to meet my friend again.

Even though we hadn't seen each other for several years, we never forgot each other. It was luck or destiny that brought us together and we became good friends again. We talked a lot and exchanged ideas about our future education. When I went inside his room and looked around I was amazed. The walls were covered in diplomas, including an English one. We had a great time together so after that we kept in touch – he would often come up to visit me in Chiang Mai or I would go to Bangkok.

A turning point came in our lives in 1992 when we each faced the challenge of going on a journey to follow our dreams. I heard that my friend Somchai Jai-in had left the monkhood. He decided to walk out of the temple to leap into a new challenge by working as a tour guide in Chiang Mai. It made me feel excited and want to try to do the same. This thought kept floating around in my head until finally I made the decision to no longer be a monk and focus on my goal of a new way of life. My dream was to look for a job so that I could earn some money to help support my parents. I also heard the good news that Somboon had passed the entrance exam to study at Chiang Mai University and had also decided to leave the monkhood. In that year, most of my friends stopped being monks including Wichai Kawichai who had passed the exam to become a police officer.

I had the opportunity to visit Somboon in Bangkok in May 1992 after he had left the temple. There was political unrest there and my friends and I joined the protests. People were protesting for General Suchinda Kraprayoon to retire as Prime Minister. We were among the angry protesters shouting in order to get Mr Suchinda to leave. One night there was a clash between military personnel and Somboon and I closely escaped death. I heard gunfire and sometimes I had to lie down on the ground, feeling bullets fly over my head. Eventually Somboon and I got separated while trying to run away from the area. When we met up again, both of us were okay. I asked him how he felt about the situation and he said that in the moment he had lost his mind and could not control his emotions because he felt the same way as the other protesters. Later he calmed down and realized that life still had many opportunities ahead. He still had parents and siblings waiting for his success at university.

During our first experience of our new lifestyle after leaving the temple we had nearly lost our lives. Somboon and I lost touch again until many years later when we found each other online. We met up and told stories from our past, happy to see each other again.

Life is a challenge!

The Trekking Guide ชีวิตซ่าไกด์ทัวร์ป่า

Chapter 4 - Life is a Destiny

A dramatic new life was about to start for me. One day I was contacted by Somchai Jai-in, my friend, who said that the tour company he worked for had jobs available. I didn't hesitate and rushed to apply and was accepted. I remember well the name - Atlantic Pacific Tours. Mr Suchart Poonsiri was the owner and he had permission to set up a tour information desk inside Chiang Mai International airport. This company changed my life and was the beginning of my tour guide career. In 1992, few people could speak a foreign language and anyone who did could work as a tour guide.

At this tour company, besides Somchai I also met a few new friends who had graduated from Thammarat Suksa School in Wat Phra Singh - Payub Ariya, Chamroen Khamtaeja and Noppadon Ruangdet. We worked as a team to help and support each other and Somchai and I rented a small room together.

Every day we went to the airport for work. Our job was to check the arrivals of all flights from Bangkok and Phuket and wait for foreign tourists. Our main duty was to give information and recommend accommodation and sightseeing tours to tourists and we had to try hard to persuade them to make a booking with us. We had contacts at a lot of hotels and guesthouses.

When passengers left the arrivals hall they walked past our tour counter. Then our challenge was to break the ice by saying "Hello, what can I help you with?" and so on to begin our negotiations. Our motto was "Whatever you want we can do for you".

The excitement and challenge had begun. It's not easy to be able to talk to a foreigner and get them to agree to a payment on the first meeting. In this case, we and the tourists had different purposes. We were the ones who gave information and offered advice for their convenience and they got what they needed from us so both sides, tourists and guides, were happy.

I still remember well those days. At first, I was very stressed and made a lot of mistakes - everything seemed too difficult. I thought it was because I had lived in a temple as a monk for a long time. Everything seemed new to me and I wasn't used to it.

When I think back to the past I can't stop laughing at my actions at that time. I was so nervous and had no confidence. I always consoled myself by thinking positively and telling myself that some things take time to learn and get used to.

I later saw a clip on YouTube of Ajarn Chalermchai Kositpipat, the man who built the famous White Temple in Chiang Rai. He said that if your heart is strong you will survive, but if your heart is weak you will lose. You must fight and fight and not give up easily and in the end you will be a winner.

An old saying goes 'hard work never killed a man'. For this reason I tried my best. The difficult part of working for this company was that there was no salary. The thing you needed to do to make money was to sell accommodation and you would get commission on the sale. When you got a chance to talk to a customer you had to do your best to make sure you got a payment. If sometimes your mission was unsuccessful, that meant no money in your pocket. That's what we did for a living.

During that time, travel was booming and a huge number of tourists from all around the world came to visit Thailand. There weren't so many tour companies and online communication was not like today. It was difficult and complicated for tourists to book a room and tour service in those days. Therefore, as freelance tour guides, we had enough work to earn a living.

The landscape of Northern Thailand is a combination of high mountains and forests and beautiful waterfalls and caves and the weather is cooler than in Bangkok. In addition, there is the charm of the northern way of life, consisting of indigenous people and various hilltribes living together harmoniously. Visitors enjoy the generosity and hospitality of the Lanna people and a wide variety of delicious northern-style food.

Chiang Mai, founded by King Mengrai the Great, was the capital of the Lanna Kingdom from 1296 until 1558. It had its own unique languages, cultures and traditions. This special city is popular with people around the world. One of the main tourist attractions is Wat Phra That Doi Suthep. This temple has a unique Lanna-style pagoda that stands high on Doi Suthep mountain. When you are up there, you can look down at the beauty of the scenery around Chiang Mai city.

There are more than three hundred temples in Chiang Mai and its colourful and beautiful Lanna architecture is known around the world. Bo Sang San Kamphaeng village is the centre of arts and crafts with Thai silk, umbrella making, silverware, lacquerware and wood carving. There are many factories to visit lined up on both sides of the Chiang Mai - San Kamphaeng road. This lively city has a lot of bars and live music and by night you can see traditional dancing shows with Northern Thai food (khan tok dinner). The Night Bazaar is a colourful market selling local and hilltribe products. Many people, both Thai and foreign, want to visit this area once in their lifetime.

Thirty years ago, one of the most popular natural attractions that Chiang Mai guides took tourists to was the beautiful Doi Inthanon, the highest mountain in Thailand. It has many beautiful waterfalls such as Mae Klang, Mae Ya, Wachiratarn, and also walking trails.

We also organised trips to Mae Rim district where there were many elephant camps such as Pong Yang elephant training camp, as well as butterfly and orchid farms and the Mae Sa waterfall. The elephant camp and river rafting area of Moo Baan Mae Ta Man village, in Mae Taeng district, was another place we visited. Then there was Tham Luang Chiang Dao cave and the Chiang Dao elephant camp. At the Chiang Mai and Myanmar border at Moo Baan Tha Ton village, you could take a long-tail boat or bamboo houseboat to see the beautiful nature along the Maekok river to Chiang Rai city. A trip to visit Mae Hong Son and Chiang Rai city was another tour that we offered to tourists at that time.

The Trekking Guide ชีวิตข้าไกด์ทัวร์ป่า

Every day I sat on the back of a friend's motorcycle, sometimes with Somchai and sometimes with Noppadon, to go to work at the airport. I didn't have my own motorcycle then which reminds me that my first job as a tour guide was full of difficulties. I was a bit disappointed. Everything was different to what I had imagined when I'd seen that tour guide at the Golden Triangle when I was younger - the man who arrived in a big bus with many tourists surrounding him, looking so dignified.

For me it was hard struggling to survive from day to day and when I asked some friends how I could get in and work for those big companies they told me that most of them were linked to tour companies abroad. Travellers booked package tours in advance and it wasn't easy to work for these companies unless you had connections.

So, now I understood that nothing is easy to come by. I said to myself that at least I could be proud of myself. I had overcome various obstacles to reach my dreams. Now I could work as a guide and speak foreign languages and earn my own money. From then on, I decided that the future was a matter of destiny and fate and I wouldn't worry about what might happen.

To work for the tourist counter at the airport we needed to be brave and not shy. When we had an opportunity to talk to customers, we had to complete the deal as quicky as possible and then find the next target. I myself had one advantage, that is that I am a cheerful person and smile easily. This was a technique which I used for work. I think smiling and a good attitude sometimes helps with this kind of service work. Even though we didn't know each other, a smiling face could help relax the atmosphere and make customers happy.

If negotiations were successful, we felt more confident and the next time was easier. I don't think I am a good salesperson, but I know myself well - I'm a humble, open-minded and honest person. The idea of taking advantage of customers didn't enter my head. Every day at work I told myself to think good and do good so that good things would follow. So, there was enough work and enough money for day-to-day spending.

Sometimes work could be very easy. Whatever you offered, the customers agreed to it. But other times, no matter what you suggested, it was rejected. You really can't take anything for granted in this world. I worked for this company for almost two years. I gained experience by taking travellers to visit various places around Chiang Mai, Chiang Rai and Mae Hong Son and this gave me the confidence to face new challenges.

In 1994 I had the opportunity to do a trekking tour for the first time. Trekking tours were famous for many years before I started working as a guide in this company, but I had never had the chance to do one. There were not many trekking companies in Chiang Mai in those days, but demand for jungle tours was increasing every year.

My friend Somchai had done a few trekking tours and created a tour brochure which he left at our workplace. He had told me about trekking tours and it made me curious and want to try because they sounded so exciting to me.

One day, I happened to pick up a brochure and show it to a customer. It turned out that I was able to sell that trekking trip even though I had never done it before - I was so surprised! I had simply tried talking to the customer about the tour using words that I had heard from friends.

I clearly remember that my first trekking clients were two middle-aged women from Switzerland. They agreed to go on a two-day one-night trip. I was so excited to be doing it, but I was also quite concerned because it was my first time. I talked to some friends who had been trekking to get as much information as I could.

The destination we led tourists to was a large jungle in a remote hilltribe area with elephant riding and bamboo rafting - you never knew what might happen. I was nervous so the day before I left, I begged my friend who had already been trekking in this area to come along with me, which gave me a little peace of mind.

I still remember well my first trek which was in the popular Mae Taeng area. I was fascinated by the thrill and challenge of living in the wild. Life had a vibrant feeling that I had never experienced before. The simplicity of the hilltribe way of life and the beauty of nature have been etched in my heart ever since.

The Trekking Guide   ชีวิตข้าไกด์ทัวร์ป่า

On the first day, we collected our clients from their hotel by pickup truck and drove to the start of the trekking route, stopping on the way at Mae Malai market to buy some necessities for our trip. After shopping, we stopped to see a beautiful waterfall which fell from a high cliff and then carried on by car to see some natural hot springs. From there we continued along the villagers' trail to Moo Baan Pha Khao Lam, a Karen hilltribe village, where we stayed overnight. We had a great time walking for three hours through incredible jungle and mountains, past Moo Baan Pong Noi Karen village to Moo Baan Pla Kluai Karen village where the tourists did a two-hour elephant ride to our overnight destination of Moo Baan Pha Khao Lam village.

While the tourists travelled by elephant, my friend and I went ahead on foot in order to find a place to stay. However, we got lost and couldn't find our way to the village. We wandered around for quite some time until we got lucky and met a villager who was cutting wood in the area. He gave us directions and we finally arrived when it was almost evening. By then, the tourists had been there for a long time, and I guessed they might be worried. I apologized and said that we had stopped to chat with a villager instead of telling the truth that we had got lost (haha!).

In the evening we cooked a Thai meal and after dinner we played games and chatted about the hilltribe people's way of life and other things. On the last day we did bamboo rafting on the Mae Taeng river which was exciting and great fun because of the rapids.

My first trekking trip left an impression on me. I had so much fun and gained a lot of experience even though we got lost in the jungle. What makes me passionate about trekking is being close to nature and being able to show various skills to tourists. It's completely different to a city tour. Experiencing the simple lives of hilltribe people reminded me of my childhood. To me it was such a happy experience that is hard to describe. My passion for trekking has stayed with me and I still think about it today.

Life is a destiny!

Chapter 5 - Life is a Pleasure

It is not easy to understand why we are born. People are born in this world into many different circumstances. We can't compare our lives with other people's ways and situations - each one is different. There can be a big gap between rich and poor which can cause confusion about the true value of life.

During our lives we all feel happiness, suffering, joy and sorrow. These feelings are caused by love, greed, anger and delusion which are all part of the everyday lives of all people, whether they are rich or poor.

I have read the life stories of many billionaires who have been successful in business and become very rich. When they reach the peak of their success many of them have similar thoughts, that is, they don't know what to do with their money. Some of them donate to charity in order to help fellow human beings, which is admirable. But often they say the same thing, that they are nostalgic for the past and that if they could turn back time, they would like to enjoy life doing the things that they wanted to do but didn't have the time for due to their work and responsibilities. At that time they had to be dedicated and committed to their careers.

For a big part of their lives they devoted too much of themselves to working towards success. Then time passed quickly and their youth was gone. Yes, they might be accomplished in their careers, but the time to do what they wanted has gone and when they finally have the time they can't because of their physical condition. They may have wealth, but their body may not support them like before. Money can't buy youth and you can't hire someone to get sick in your place. Therefore, when you're young if you want to do something you should hurry up and do it, don't delay.

Sometimes we must break the rules of life. Life is not a machine, sometimes we have to ignore the rules in order to have some fun. We must be true to ourselves, but not give up on our goals. Too much of anything is not good.

According to an interesting book I read, there are two goals in one's life - the first goal is career success and the second goal is happiness. For the first goal, as long as we know what we want we can focus on our target and try to reach it through trial and error. Finding the way to success is not difficult if we don't give up. Someday success will be ours.

But the second goal, happiness, is difficult to reach because it is an abstract thing that can't be captured. Not everyone's idea of happiness is the same, therefore it's impossible to define what happiness is. It's not an achievement that can be maintained over time, it sometimes disappears and the more we chase it the more it flies away from us, just like a mosquito. If we run after it, it will fly away, but sometimes if we just sit still, it will come to us. Happiness is just a feeling and an illusion, but many people say that success brings happiness.

In this competitive world, people have to fight to be successful. They try to do whatever it takes to be a winner, in order to obtain wealth and satisfy the craving for material gain. Sometimes people even do bad things just to obtain power and wealth to satisfy their desires. Can people be happy without money? Buddha said that true happiness is peace in your mind, do you believe that?

Does a lot of money really make people happy? There are many stories about rich families where the husband and wife divorce and the family splits up. Siblings fight over wealth even if they already have a lot of money. Indeed, having a big house and an expensive car is not always a guarantee that one's life will be peaceful. One may be financially comfortable, but inside the mind there is no real peace.

Life is like a burning candle. We know that one day it will go out, but we don't know how or when that will happen. Maybe a wind will blow it out prematurely or something will fall on it causing the flame to be extinguished. Sometimes this candle may be fortunate enough to be able to maintain its glow until the end of its predetermined time. We humans are not born to find the meaning of life, we are born to live a meaningful life. In this world, our actions, good or bad, are our choice. Nobody forces us to do things. What other people do to you is their karma (both good and bad actions), but what you choose to do is your karma. Don't worry too much about other people's stories. We arrive on this earth alone and ultimately we die alone.

After my experience of that first trekking tour, my attitude changed slightly. Money and wealth may be important, but won't always make us happy. I used to dream of becoming a guide, working for big companies and earning a lot of money to live a luxurious life. I imagined this lifestyle when I was still a novice, but my first trekking tour changed my way of thinking. The old thoughts slowly faded away and I discovered what kind of person I was and I knew what I wanted to do. True happiness is not only about money, knowing our true self is vital. I wanted to work and live closer to nature and meet people from different countries, so trekking tours were the answer for me. I was lucky to see and experience the simple way of life of the hilltribe people and a lot of things became clear to me.

Now I knew what my idea of happiness was - to do what I love and be able to earn a living and take care of my parents. To try to be a good person in society without causing trouble to anyone, that's my goal.

Life is a pleasure!

The Trekking Guide ชีวิตข้าไกด์ทัวร์ป่า

Chapter 6 - The Trekking Guide

The Thai master monk Luang Phor Buddhadasa said we shouldn't expect too much from life because nothing is certain. The destination we are walking towards sometimes depends on fate. There are many unforeseen events that we can't explain. Someone's life can change just by reading one good book or because an unexpected incident occurred. Sometimes we may be unaware that our destiny is chosen by God.

One day things may happen because destiny has already drawn a path for us. This was the case with the tour company that we worked for. The company's owner didn't receive permission to renew the rental contract in Chiang Mai International Airport so he had to close the business down. I and all my friends who worked there had to leave suddenly and look for new jobs - life must go on.

Somchai and I had both wanted to work as trekking guides. We applied for a job at one of the small guesthouses which ran a jungle tour business in Chiang Mai. Here was a challenge in the battlefield of my life once again and this was my dream job.

SSS guesthouse was located near Chiang Mai Physical Education College outside the city centre. It was a large wooden house on two floors; the ground floor was built with cement and the second floor was all wood. There were more than twenty rooms to accommodate tourists costing 150 baht per night. It was one of many similar guesthouses in Chiang Mai that were popular with tourists at that time.

I'm not sure how and when trekking tours began. I asked a friend of mine, Mr Pinit Inthapan, who was a trekking guide. This man was well known among friends as guide Nit. He wore glasses and had long hair which was a popular style at that time. He told me that jungle tours happened by chance; some nature-loving tourists wanted an adventure so they hired a guide to help them take a trip up into the mountains to spend a night there with hilltribe people.

There are many hilltribe villages in the jungle of Northern Thailand including the Karen, Lahu, Akha, Lisu, Hmong, Yao and Pha Long. They have a simple lifestyle and have been hidden in the jungle for a long time. The different ethnic groups each have their own language and cultural diversity but their way of life is similar - they believe in mystical spirits and the spirits of their deceased ancestors.

A lot of Karen people live along the Burmese border and lead a distinctive way of life in the forest. They grow their crops on terraces and raise animals in order to be self-sufficient. The Hmong, Lisu and Yao hilltribes migrated from southern China and have a similar lifestyle to each other, as can be seen from their clothing and housing, preferring to live in cold highlands. Their way of life is rotation farming and raising small animals such as pigs and chickens for consumption and rituals. The Lahu and Akha hilltribes originate from the land of Tibet and their way of life is similar to the Hmong, Lisu and Yao.

When tourists experienced the beauty of nature and the simple way of life unique to the hilltribes it touched their hearts. Word of it spread and more and more people wanted to visit. Since then, there has been a demand for jungle tours which has opened the tourism market and led to the growth of tour companies and accommodation services in Chiang Mai. Trekking guides were pioneers of a new way of adventure travel in nature.

Now I'd like to tell you some funny stories about friends who I worked with at SSS guesthouse, the place that inspired me to become a professional jungle tour guide.

In this guesthouse we all lived together like brothers. The joint owners of the business were Mr Somsak Malee, Mr Dam, Mr Kang and Mr Kuwa. Mr Somchai was the driver and Miss Saiyud was the chef. My trekking guide friends were Mr Boontan, Mr Ninja, Mr Serm, Mr Udon, Mr Butt, Mr Simi, Mr Sinchai, Mr Tee and Mr Somchai Jai-in. We were allowed to share one big room and everyone chose a corner to sleep in. If you had money, you could rent a private room and come in to work every day. Some people lived in their own homes, but people who had nowhere to stay could live at the guesthouse for free.

We described ourselves as crazy jungle boys who lived a life of fun. We mocked each other by saying "Eat like a pig, sleep like a bear". Every morning the chef cooked a big pot of food and we found a plate, put rice on it and food on top and sat and ate together like pigs and when it was time for bed we each slept in our corner of the room, just like hibernating bears.

I was excited to be able to live like this again as it reminded me of when I was a novice at the temple. We had a lot of fun and good laughs, eating and drinking together and supporting each other.

Our main duty was to wake up early in the morning to pick up tourists who travelled by budget bus from Bangkok. There were companies in various locations around Khao San Road that sold bus tickets to tourists who wanted to come to Chiang Mai.

Each guesthouse had its own guide and driver waiting to persuade tourists to stay at their guesthouse. When the buses arrived and the tourists got off, each trekking guide would try to show them pictures of the guesthouse that they worked in. It was a competition between trekking guides to use their presenting skills to get tourists to stay at their guesthouse. Anyone who had a great strategy or magic words was able to convince tourists to go with them. If they went back without tourists, neither the owners nor the guides were happy.

Whenever tourists agreed to stay with us, we took them back to the guesthouse, gave them tourist information and tried to sell the trekking tours which were run by the guesthouse. The tour could be four days three nights, three days two nights or two days one night depending on what the tourists wanted.

Another duty was waiting on tables and taking food and drink orders from customers and making them feel comfortable. It allowed us to learn more languages as well because we were around tourists almost every day.

We noticed that most trekking tourists preferred to do the three-day two-night programme because it wasn't too long. Every day the guides took turns to lead a trek. For example, at the guesthouse where I worked there were a total of seven guides and we had to form a queue. We decided who was first in the queue, then who was second and so on. We agreed between us that the first guide in the queue must be at the guesthouse to take care of customers all day on the day before his trek. That way he could try to get as many customers as possible - the more customers you got, the more profit you made.

The SSS guesthouse three-day two-night programme followed a route from Mae Wang to Mae Chaem via Doi Inthanon National Park with the highest mountain in Thailand. We called this route Mae Na Jon because the last day of the journey out of the jungle ended at Ban Mae Na Jon village in Mae Chaem District.

I got my first chance to explore the route as a porter for the guide Boontan who called himself Mr Billy. That time we had twelve clients, most of whom were British. I was very excited about this trip because I had never done this route before and I had to learn many things from Mr Boontan before being allowed to do it by myself.

On this route we travelled south from Chiang Mai city, passing through Hang Dong and San Patong districts and turning right to Mae Wang towards our destination. The vehicle that we used was a two-row pickup truck (songthaew) which had a roof rack to carry the travellers' backpacks and food that we took for the trip.

We stopped at Majomrong in the San Patong district to buy necessities that we would use in the jungle. We had to calculate how much would be required for the three-day two-night period. Mr Boontan advised the tourists to buy anything they needed here because when we hiked to the hilltribe villages there would be nowhere to shop.

Trekking tours are a valuable activity in my opinion which allow foreigners to truly see the way of life of the local people. Tourists were excited and interested when they visited the local market because it sold many things that they hadn't seen before like frogs, insects and snakes as well as exotic fruits and vegetables. They are also a way to bring income into the area.

After we finished shopping at the market, we drove through Mae Wang district and stopped for lunch at a restaurant in a small village. Then we continued the journey by car again until our destination. I guess the time from Chiang Mai by car to the village at Moo Baan Kariang Huai Khao Leeb ('Moo Baan' means 'village') was about three hours. After this we had to travel on foot through a large forest for three hours to stay overnight in another village.

In this area there were very few Karen and Hmong tribes. When we were up high and looked across the mountains it seemed as if there was no-one living there, but there were some small tribal villages hidden away. They had a simple and peaceful way of life with no electricity or facilities.

Another important person on trekking tours who we should mention is the porter. On a journey in the jungle, it was important to have local people with us who knew the area. We found a porter in Moo Baan Huai Khao Leeb (Karen village) to come with us as an assistant. The porter's duty is to know the route well, to help carry various loads, to help cook food and to make sure everyone stays safe together with the guide.

On the first day, after we had finished hiking we stayed overnight in a Hmong hilltribe village. On the second day we passed through an amazing rainforest on the way to Moo Baan Mae Mu (Karen village) where we stayed for our second night. On the third day, the tourists did an elephant ride from Moo Baan Mae Mu and then walked to a bamboo raft camp in order to do bamboo rafting on the Mae Jam river. Finally, we arrived at Moo Baan Mae Na Jon and stopped for a rest and to have lunch. At the end, our driver came to pick us up and we drove through Doi Inthanon National Park, stopping on the way to see Huai Sai Leaung waterfall.

We returned safely to the guesthouse in Chiang Mai. I had had a great time and gained a lot of experience on this trip and all the tourists seemed very happy.

Trekking tours have changed lives by creating new ways of generating income for various local communities. They have helped hilltribe children learn new things and get the chance to meet foreigners and practice foreign languages. Children of villages in remote areas were unable to access good learning resources like children in cities. I could see that many children in the villages were very clever, but they had no opportunity to study. The young men in particular had a chance to earn some money by working as porters. Many of my friends who were trekking tour guides first worked as porters to help the guides. While doing their duties, they were keen to learn to communicate in other languages and they practiced speaking with tourists. Then they progressed from being porters to proudly becoming trekking guides.

Every time I took tourists into villages, it was a great feeling to see the children having fun. I remember when we arrived at various villages and stayed overnight there the children would come running to look at the foreigners. Some of them were nervous because tourists looked strange to them. Some kids giggled and some were scared and cried because they had never seen people who looked like that before - it was hilarious!

The beauty of trekking as an activity is learning and changing the attitudes of tourists and local people - it makes an impression on tourists, guides, porters and villagers. They build good relationships with each other, even if it is only for short periods of time. People from different backgrounds spend time close to each other and it can create new perspectives and attitudes towards others, creating love, sympathy and understanding of other ways of life.

It's hard to explain what makes tourists from different cultures, different countries and who speak different languages decide to live together with the local people when sometimes they can barely communicate with each other. Throughout the past thirty years, trekking guides, porters and mahouts have married foreigners that they met during a trek. It has changed the lives of 'jungle boys' who have moved overseas to live in every corner of the world.

The charm of the trekking tour makes people fall in love - I'm not sure if it is destiny or just a coincidence.

I am a trekking guide!

Chapter 7 - Life is Blowing in the Wind

I remember when I started to work as a trekking guide. It was the best time for the jungle tour industry in my opinion. It was so popular then, with a huge number of tourists coming to visit Northern Thailand. There were many guesthouses and tour companies offering trekking tours and welcoming tourists from all over the world. When a business flourishes there will always be competition, with each guesthouse exploring a new trekking route in order to offer an alternative - if you have an interesting route that has never been travelled, it's even more intriguing to tourists and makes them want to do it.

The most famous trekking area at that time was in the northern part of Chiang Mai, in the Mae Taeng and Chiang Dao district where you can go bamboo rafting in the Mae Taeng river. Here you can find the Mok Fah waterfall and the trekking routes of Pong Diaud - Sob Kai, Lisu Huai Nam Dang - Sob Kai, Hmong Pa Kia - Sob Kai and Muang Kong - Sob Kai. All these routes finished at Sob Kai village because that's where you ended up after rafting along the Mae Taeng river and where the drivers picked up the trekkers to take them back to Chiang Mai.

Other trekking routes were Pai - Mae Hong Son, Phrao - Chiang Dao, and the Chiang Rai route was Karen Ruammit - Moo Baan Lahu Yafu. The southern Chiang Mai routes were Mae Najon - Doi Inthanon, Mae Sa-nga - Doi Inthanon, Mae Tala - Doi Inthanon, Mae Tho - Mae Chaem and Hmong Huai Nam Rin - Karen Huai Hoi and later there were many new routes around Sob Win subdistrict.

At that time, Chiang Mai was a peaceful and pleasant place to live. I still remember as if it were yesterday the atmosphere in the morning around Thapae Gate. Tour guides would drive their motorcycles around looking to hire a car and driver to pick up their tourists. As I said, there were many different trekking routes and Thapae Gate was the place where drivers would wait for guides to contact them. The atmosphere was full of fun between us as we negotiated prices to hire a car and sometimes we would share it with another tour guide if we were both going on the same trekking route.

The guesthouse owners set the conditions for the tours. They would state the price for a trek including the vehicle, three meals a day, hiking, elephant riding and bamboo rafting activities. They would take a percentage and whatever was left after expenses would be the guide's pay. So, when it came to the guide's turn to do the job, he had to find as many tourists as possible.

We had a system to help each other out in case of a low number of tourists. If a guide had to run the trip with a small number of people, he wouldn't have enough money left to pay himself so we aimed to get twelve tourists each time. If it turned out that we were unlucky and we got only four people, once the guesthouse owner had taken their percentage and we deducted the costs of hiring porters, food, transport, elephant riding, trekking and rafting activities, we hardly had any money left in our pockets.

Sometimes we had to cancel a trip and send our customers to other companies. When that happened we shared the costs with another tour guide from a different company and who also had a small number of customers. If we thought that by joining together to do a trip we might end up with enough money left in our pocket, we would do it. This system of joining tours together was often fun. If it was the turn of a guide to do a trek the next day and he didn't have enough bookings he felt a little stressed. He would drive his motorbike around to different tour offices and ask other tour guides to negotiate the best plan – either to take his customers or to join together for the tour.

There were regular jokes going on as some guides would lie to each other. For example, a tour guide might have only three customers but say that he had five. This is because whoever had the higher number had the upper hand and had more power to negotiate than the one with fewer customers. In that case he would say he'd take the other ones - it was hilarious when we found out the truth later and we always made fun of each other.

Now I'd like to share some stories about my own experiences and those of my trekking guide friends who I worked with in the past.

After I got a job as a trekking guide at SSS guesthouse I had the opportunity to lead a three-day two-night tour along the Mae Najon - Doi Inthanon route for the first time. This was a non-touristic route which no company other than SSS guesthouse did. I was so excited and remembered everything I had done as a trainee on this route with Mr Boontan. This was my time to shine, I had to manage everything by myself. There were ten people in total - European, American and Japanese.

On the evening before the trip, I had to organise a meeting with them to share some information and give everyone the chance to get to know each other before we spent time together in the jungle. One important thing I had to do was to compile a list of who would travel with me on this trip and I had to report all this information to the tourist police with details about the area that we would will travel to.

I introduced myself by saying "Hello everyone, my name is Yao and I am the guide for you guys on this trip and I will try to do my best". Then I followed up with advice about what necessary things they would need to bring and a few tips on dos and don'ts for when we were in the hilltribe villages. The atmosphere was fun and full of laughter.

The next morning, after breakfast, we set off on our journey south of Chiang Mai to our first stop at Majomrong market in San Patong district. Then we stopped for lunch and continued to Huai Khao Lieb, a Karen village, at which point our car journey ended. The drive up and down the narrow and winding mountain road could be quite dangerous. When it rained the road was wet, muddy and slippery. At one point the car got stuck in the mud and I had to ask the tourists to get out and help me push it. It was fun and at the end we were all laughing about the mud on our hands and clothes.

When we arrived at the village I found a porter whose name was Phatee Kaew (Patee). In the Karen language this means 'uncle'. I hired him to help carry loads and take care of safety alongside me as well as leading as a local guide. We helped each other to pack all the food in our backpacks and were ready to go for an adventure in the jungle. We hiked up and down through beautiful surroundings. Everywhere we looked it was lush and green because it was the rainy season.

When we arrived at Moo Baan Hmong Huai Yen, I asked to stay with one of the Hmong families who allowed tourists and we stayed in a typical Hmong house. I'll try to explain the unique style of this simple house as it was then. The walls were made of wood and bamboo and there was no flooring, just the earth. The living area was at ground level. This area was divided into three parts – the bedroom in one corner of the room slept a family of four, the main area was for receiving visitors and storing belongings and there was a kitchen with a fire on the ground for cooking.

With permission from the owner, I took my ten tourists to stay in the house. I took a large plastic mat that the villagers used to dry rice and crops and put it on the ground in the living area to provide a space like a dorm room. Everyone lying in a row, with blankets and pillows, was the best you could get in the jungle – "Welcome to this five-star hotel, we don't allow snoring!" I joked and it made everyone laugh. It was a once-in-a-lifetime experience for these tourists who were used to sleeping in comfortable hotels in the city. Now they had to sleep in the middle of the jungle in a small village and live like simple forest dwellers. At night there were no electric lights so it was pitch black and we had to find our way to bed by candlelight.

In the evening no-one took a shower because the weather on the mountain is very cold and there was no toilet or bathroom. Uncle Kaew and I helped each other to light a fire, boil water and make tea and coffee to serve to the tourists and then we cooked dinner for them. Whatever I cooked they would say it was delicious, I guess because they were tired from travelling. After dinner, we sat and talked about our day while sipping moonshine whiskey to keep away the cold. At dawn we listened to the sound of pigs and chickens as the villagers set them free to find food. They would come back late in the evening to sleep near their owner's house.

The most annoying thing at night was if anyone had a stomach-ache and wanted to go to the bathroom because the toilets weren't at all luxurious. On this trip, there were two Japanese women in the group. One of them, named Miki, went out to do her 'business' in the early morning in the bushes behind the house. I heard a scream and she came running to me. When I asked her what the matter was, she replied that while sitting down to do her business a huge black pig had come along and bitten her on the behind! In shock, she ran and cried for help. I said, "Everything's fine and you're safe". I knew there was no danger - I guessed the villagers' pigs were looking around for food in the early morning and were surprised by her.

When everyone was awake, Uncle Kaew and I prepared tea, coffee and breakfast for everyone while chatting about Miki's encounter with the pig. There was a couple from Holland in the group - the woman's name was Helena and she was travelling with her husband. She said that she went to do her business the evening before and while doing so, a dog stood and stared. She tried to shoo it away, but it wouldn't go so she lost the need to go. I suggested that if anyone needed to do their business it was safer to take a friend. I joked that next time you want to go to the toilet, you should organise a 'toilet party'!

After breakfast, we prepared for our journey to Moo Baan Mae Mu, a Karen village, where we would spend the second night. We packed our belongings, saying thank you and goodbye to the owner of the house, and set off. That day we had to walk for about five to six hours through evergreen forest which connects to Doi Inthanon national park. I let Uncle Kaew lead the way and I followed.

We were ready for our adventure. While we were hiking up and downhill it was raining which made travelling twice as difficult. Some tourists who had raincoats were lucky, but those who didn't got wet clothes. We walked through the dense jungle for almost five hours without reaching our destination. I was worried so I asked Uncle Kaew if we were lost. He assured me that we were ok. He said that he had been on this route many times so I said no more and kept walking. Eventually I realised that we were lost. It was dark and the tourists began to complain about being tired and hungry.

"What's happened?" I wondered. I was apprehensive, confused and embarrassed, and swore to myself in my head - damn it! I couldn't believe that on my first trekking trip in this area we were totally lost. We continued walking and the rain was still falling with no sign of stopping. At last, we reached a point on the top of a mountain with enough space to shelter from the rain and I told the tourists that we were lost, but not to worry. I promised I would take good care of them and find the fastest way to reach the village as soon as possible.

I knew it wasn't wise to travel in the woods without light as it could be very dangerous, so I told everyone that we would stay where we were and I would find a way to get us to the village. I cut some bamboo and some dry wood to set up a large fire to warm everyone and shared enough food to satisfy everyone's hunger.

Uncle Kaew and I discussed a plan to find a way out of the jungle and he offered to go by himself which would be easier. We would wait for him here, and he would find some people from the village to take us there as quickly as possible.

Everyone tried to reassure me. An American couple in the group joked "Shit happens!" A Japanese girl came to squeeze my shoulder and said in Japanese "Don't give up". We were stuck on that mountain until almost 9pm when, from the dark, a light emerged and we heard the voices of five or six villagers along with the light from their bamboo torches. We were all overjoyed.

Slowly helping each other, we walked down the mountain following the torches of the villagers until we could see the village in front of us. I looked at my watch, it was almost midnight!

When we arrived at Moo Baan Mae Mu village, almost all the villagers, including children and adults, came to stand and look at the cold, wet trekking guide who had got lost in the jungle, it was so embarrassing.

On the last day of that trip, after breakfast, the tourists rode elephants to the bamboo rafting camp. Then we walked a short distance to the Mae Jam river and spent over two hours rafting to reach Moo Baan Mae Najon where we stopped for lunch and the driver came to pick us up. Everything went well that day. We stopped to see a waterfall along the way and got back to Chiang Mai safely.

When we arrived at the guesthouse I was a little apprehensive that the tourists would complain, but it turned out that I was fortunate that no one blamed me for the incident in the jungle. On the contrary, everyone was willing to give me a small tip while jokingly saying to me "Thank you very much for getting me lost in the jungle!". And that evening, a Japanese girl invited me out on a date to have dinner with her. I thought to myself if I knew that would happen, I would pretend to get lost on every trip - haha!

Life is just like the wind of change, you never know what's going to happen. The wind of fortune will blow something to you. It continues to blow both day and night and it's hard to predict where it will take you. What will the wind of life bring to you?

Life is blowing in the wind!

The Trekking Guide ชีวิตข้าไกด์ทัวร์ป่า

Chapter 8 - Life is Fun

The popularity of trekking tourism has not declined since those days. There are still a lot of tourists from all over the world travelling to Thailand, especially to Chiang Mai and the north, for that reason. Trekking doesn't require much preparation - as long as you are fit, adventurous and enjoy being close to nature, that's enough.

The tourism industry grew quickly over a period of ten years. If you wandered around Chiang Mai you would see more and more foreigners from western Europe, America and Japan walking side by side. There were so many guesthouses, bars, souvenir shops, traditional Thai massage parlours and car rental shops popping up like mushrooms all over the city.

It created new jobs and income for people who lived in rural areas thanks to the trekking routes that passed through there. It was a good time for trekking guides, shopkeepers, villagers and anyone whose business was linked to trekking tours, many people benefited from the money that came from tourists.

Why are names important? A lot of trekking guides changed their names either deliberately, so that tourists could easily remember them, or by accident when tourists mis-pronounced them. For example, one of my friends whose name is Jamnong got the nickname 'James' and Mr Serm got the name 'Sam'. Mr Sarnit, a porter, became 'Sunny' and Mr Simaun became 'Simon'. Mr Boontan changed his name to 'Billy' and Mr Jarun called himself 'Bob' because he liked Bob Marley. My best friend, Somchai Jai-in, changed his name to 'Otto', Sinchai To-a changed to 'ET' and Mr Nirun Muang Kham was nicknamed Tee so he called himself 'Mr T'. As I am a tall person, many of my friends called me Yao which means 'tall man', so I got the name 'Yao Jungle Boy'.

A lot of trekking guides also liked to name themselves after well-known movie characters, for example, the movie Rambo was popular in those days with the main character being a strong man with big muscles so guide Suphot and Uncle Sawat, a senior trekking guide, both called themselves 'Rambo'. Mr Nut, a porter from Muang Kong, called himself 'Coconut Dundee', based on the movie Crocodile Dundee.

All these trekking guides who I have mentioned were legends at that time and they had many funny stories to tell. Thirty years ago, most of us learned languages directly from tourists while guiding them on trips. Our language knowledge was very limited and sometimes we had to use sign language. I remember porters trying to memorise and copy every word the guides said and often they would take on the personality and style of their guide.

It was often tricky and amusing when we tried to communicate with tourists and there were lots of jokes among guides who teased each other about their language skills. You might see funny phrases printed on t-shirts sold in Khao San Road or the Night Bazaar market, it makes us proud that some of them originated from trekking guides. For example, the expression "Same same but different" has a funny origin. Once, a guide was asked by tourists "What's the difference between the Karen and Lahu hilltribes?". The guide didn't know how to answer so he just said that they're the same same but different! (He wanted to say they are quite similar). And sometimes guides teased the tourists. When we travelled in the jungle and tourists were shocked by something, they often exclaimed "Oh my God!". The guide made fun of them by saying, "Oh My Buddha!" - that was hilarious!

One day some tourists were taking a photo of a tour guide and porter and tried to get their attention by saying "Look!". But in Thai 'look' means 'stand up'. It turns out that the guide and porter were already standing up so they were very confused!

A lot of trekking guides like to drink alcohol. When we drink whiskey, we feel that we can speak the language better and we are more confident. There was a funny incident that happened to a senior guide, Uncle Sawat Rambo, and his porter, Coconut Dundee, that we liked to laugh about. Apparently, the two of them took a German couple on a tour along the Pong Daud - Sob Kai route. Uncle Sawat Rambo was a person who liked to drink alcohol and his porters were no different due to learning and practicing English with him and everything he said, the porters had to agree with.

By chance, the German couple also liked to drink alcohol so it was a perfect match and they all travelled together happily. On the first day they started drinking in the morning. Then they stopped to buy essentials and some more alcohol at Mae Malai market - by that time the guide and porter believed that they were fluent in English and German. They continued drinking together for the rest of the car journey until they arrived at their drop-off point, then they continued on foot uphill towards the Karen village.

By now everyone was very drunk and because of that they couldn't keep up with each other along the mountain path to the village. There were many confusing crossroads and in the end the guide got lost in one place, the porter got lost in another place and the tourists were lost somewhere else! The people of the village had to go looking for them and managed to find them just before dark.

I often met Uncle Sawat Rambo and guide Suphot Rambo when we trekked on the same route. One time I was taking tourists on a three-day two-night jungle trip on the Mae Tang route and I met Suphot Rambo on the second night when we stayed at a village belonging to the Lahu tribe. If we met other trekking guides in the village where we were staying, we would help each other out and share things. That evening I ran out of coffee so I went to ask guide Suphot Rambo if I could borrow some. I arrived at the house where he was staying and found him sitting there talking to the tourists and pouring local whiskey from a bottle into a glass, "This is moonshine whiskey, it's very good for you!", he said. I could see him downing it and saying "Yeah, very good". Then he poured another glass and passed it to a young man in the group who drank it and said, "Oh! It's very strong Rambo!". Guide Suphot Rambo looked pleased with himself and laughed.

Later I heard the young man ask guide Suphot, "Hey Rambo, today we were supposed to visit a cave, but we didn't see it. What happened?". He kept asking and finally, because he wasn't able to explain the real reason in English, guide Suphot just replied, "Oh, sorry! The cave has moved - ha!" The young foreigner was baffled by this answer and I guess he was a little disappointed.

The life of a trekking guide is a life of happiness and fun, but without money. Our income depends on each tour and it's not as stable as full-time work with a salary each month. It's a simple life spent close to nature. We have to work no matter what season it is in all kinds of weather.

It's not suitable for anyone who wants to be rich, but I feel very happy to have had this career. Maybe I wasn't able to work in a comfortable air-conditioned office doing a well-respected job, but the joy and experience I gained can't be bought with money. In this career, we meet many people from all over the world and being responsible for them during a tour is a challenge that tests our abilities. We get to know and make friends with people from overseas while doing fun and exciting activities and sometimes we become good friends.

There is always a risk of danger while travelling in the forest and when doing activities such as elephant riding and bamboo rafting, we can't guarantee that there will be no accidents Sometimes an elephant goes crazy and chases its mahout. Tourists and guides have been injured and some have even died. Bamboo rafting in the raging river during the rainy season can be dangerous. The raft can be swallowed up by the river or break apart.

To be a trekking guide you must love nature and be patient. The unfamiliar climate and environment mean some tourists can't carry their luggage so the trekking guides and porters must be ready to help. This is one of their charms that maybe appeals to foreign girls!

Trekking guides used to wear their hair long, down to the middle of their backs, like western musicians of the 1970s and 1980s. Any guide with long hair was a favourite of western girls, especially one who could play the guitar and sing western songs – he would get a lot of attention! In those days most of my friends had long hair. I was the only person who didn't. I'm not sure why, maybe because I thought it would be hard work to take care of? I don't know.

In the evening after a trek, guides would ride their motorbikes around the city with a foreign girl sitting on the back, showing off at the Chiang Mai pubs where live music was playing. If you were a trekking guide or a porter on a motorcycle with a foreign girl on the back, you were cool! The favourite places to go drinking were The Old West pub, Riverside pub and Brasserie. Mr Tuk of Brasserie was one of the legendary musicians at that time. After a tour, we would take tourists to celebrate at these bars and sometimes we went there with friends as single men to hang out with foreign girls.

It was the trekking guide's job to ensure safety and cook meals during the trip. Each one had their own individual personality, but for the main duties guides copied senior guides from generation to generation. For example, when cooking food for tourists in the evening, I'm certain that each of them made soup, Thai green curry, stir-fried vegetables and sweet and sour chicken. They would repeat these four dishes every trip. As for international music, I'm sure every guide was able to sing the song 'Take me home country road' by John Denver. On each trek, while walking up and down mountains, everyone would be singing "Country road, take me home, to the place I belong, West Virginia, mountain mama, take me home, country road" and laughing and having a lot of fun together.

When it came to the special skill of winning the hearts of foreign girls, everyone had their own unique way that couldn't be imitated, but those who could play the guitar and sing well had a better chance than others.

One of the most popular guides among young western girls at that time was Mr Sinchai To-A, or 'ET' as he called himself. This young Karen man from Muang Kong village, Chiang Dao district, originally worked as a porter for many guides who took tourists through his village. He learned and practiced languages by himself until he proudly became a trekking guide.

I myself was not so popular because I preferred alcohol! I sometimes tried a simple technique though. In the evening while cooking dinner, if I liked a girl I would invite her to come and help me in the kitchen. This allowed me to show off my cooking skills and impress her, but whether she liked me or not was in the hands of Cupid. Sometimes my plan didn't work because she preferred the porter. Ha!

As trekking guides we had freedom and a lot of fun at work. We had a good balance - we would be close to nature and experience life in the jungle for a few days then we would come back and stay in the city. Alternating like this worked well for me.

When we weren't leading a tour, we would drink with friends in the guesthouse, playing the guitar and singing together to try to get the attention of foreign girls who were staying there. Life was full of laughter. Sometimes a foreign girl became a girlfriend. We always joked with each other that if you had a foreign girlfriend, it meant you had won the lottery. It was a simple life, but a great feeling to be a trekking guide. Some people might be rich or famous - I don't care. That life was enough for me.

Life is fun!

Chapter 9 - Life is Always Changing

I continued my life as a tour guide because of the fun, excitement and joy in this job. It was enough to earn a living and sometimes I had enough money left to help support my parents. Gratitude towards my mother and father has always been in my heart.

I took tourists trekking in many areas, hiking through mountains, rivers and hilltribe villages around Chiang Mai, Chiang Rai and Mae Hong Son. I can't remember how many hundreds of times I served as a jungle tour guide. Time flies so fast that sometimes we can barely remember what we have done. There are good times and bad times. I remember some occasions when I nearly died, for example, when swimming across a river to reach an elephant camp to find the mahout. Another time, I was steering a bamboo raft and it crashed into rocks. I jumped into the water to try to push it away and the strong current dragged me down the river. I managed to swim to the bank and then I had to get back to the raft to save the tourists, but by that time I had almost run out of breath.

For many people, a good job means working for a company with a good reputation, job security and a decent salary as well as a nice house and car in order to show off your social status. None of this is guaranteed if you are a trekking guide, but I feel fortunate to have done this job. For me a good quality of life was more satisfying than wealth. We can choose to be happy in our own way without having to follow the values of society.

I'm afraid that one day soon the simple and peaceful way of life in the villages will change. Greedy and selfish behaviour exists in all societies and money and objects have more value than morals. The madness of materialism is what destroys the simple way of life in communities.

Technological progress is leading to change. Good morals and customs of the past are being destroyed by the worship of money and objects. New generations are attracted by what they see on TV and don't want to listen to their parents and grandparents who led a simpler life and were content with just enough to support their families and relatives. The traditional peace of self-sufficiency and mutual support between relatives is disappearing.

Every time I went on a trip to experience the lives of the villagers, I saw the beauty of a pure and simple life and I didn't want my visits with foreign tourists to have an impact on that. Sometimes I felt sad and guilty about bringing new things into their communities, like cameras and mobile phones.

In big cities people are not always honest with each other. Life is fast-paced and you have to battle and compete to gain power, status and money. People boast about being richer, better and more important than others. Wherever prosperity is gained there will be change. Obtaining as much money and as many possessions as possible becomes the most important goal. We become fascinated by a new life that requires money without stopping to think that before we had these things, we were happy even so. Isn't it enough just to have the necessities – food, clothing, medicine and a home that is warm and provides protection from the sun and rain?

I don't want to see the disintegration of family units in the rural communities that I visited. I want society to see and appreciate goodness and uphold justice. We should respect each other as equals even if we have different values. Acceptance and respect of each other should not be based on money and power.

We cannot avoid change; everything will change sooner or later, even our own lives and thoughts are constantly changing according to the conditions at the time. If change is to happen, I would like to see social equality without discriminating against race, skin colour or the gap between rich and poor.

All people should be equal - every life has value and meaning. We should not judge others by power and money. A person's skills should not only be measured by a degree from a famous university. Knowledge is universal, not only restricted to studies, and we can learn many different things in life through experience.

During the period that I spent with villagers and hilltribe people far from civilization and with few amenities, I saw the invaluable wisdom and traditions they inherited from their ancestors and passed down from generation to generation. I don't want to see these valuable lessons lost due to changes by the Thai government who have been trying to develop villages according to their own vision without understanding the needs of the people who live there.

Sometimes the government has tried to impose development programmes that villagers don't want because they are incompatible with their customs. I say enough is enough with the use of the power of the law to interfere with their peaceful way of life. I have heard stories of villagers who were harassed by government officials using legal channels to make unwanted changes. There are many selfish bureaucrats involved in projects who are always looking for opportunities to take advantage of villagers and use the force of the law for their own benefit.

The injustice that arises from government policy without taking into account the facts and the villagers' genuine needs is sad. They are unable to set a direction or make a development plan based on their own way of thinking.

I would like to see the government choose children from each community to study at university. When they have graduated, they can go back and use their knowledge to develop their own community. Most importantly, the government must be willing to allow villagers to have the power to decide for themselves whether or not to accept projects or policies that are presented to them.

My life as a trekking guide continued and I saw many changes and gained more experience. The path of life on jungle tours was still fascinating to follow and the road ahead was still long with many challenges to face in order to prove my abilities.

I was physically and mentally full of energy and ready to overcome many obstacles on the way to positive changes in the future because life is full of changes. Every day things change, but one thing that doesn't is the love that parents have for their children. Sometimes we need to find the opportunity to be quiet and alone so that we can let go of chaotic thoughts and reflect on our childhood and growing up.

Find the time occasionally to be with your parents to repay their love and kindness towards you - tell your mum how wonderful she is. We only have one set of parents and when one day they die, we can't replace them. On the other hand, we can replace a husband or wife if we separate. So, before we leave this world, the most important thing we should do is love and care for our parents while we have the chance to do so.

Life is always changing!

Chapter 10 - Life Must Go On

In 1992, the Tourism Authority of Thailand introduced a new law - anyone working with foreign tourists, especially tour guides, had to have a tour guide licence. Therefore, they organised a training programme that tour guides had to complete in order to be officially recognised as professionals. It was held at Chiang Mai University and I had the opportunity to do the course. It didn't require any educational qualifications. Anyone who could speak another language was eligible to attend because most trekking guides didn't have certificates or a school diploma.

Thailand had become stricter and had introduced laws and measures to control and protect the safety of tourists. At that time, the number of foreign visitors was increasing every year, but also the crime rate against tourists was getting worse which could damage the country's reputation. So, from then on, everyone who wanted to be a tour guide had to have an official licence – we called it the 'Roon Poi Phee'.

I met many new classmates and some of us are still friends today including Mr Nikom Tanava, who used to work for Enjoy Tour company and Mr Boonsong Chomphusomsa, who worked for many companies in Chiang Mai. These two friends married Japanese women. Mr Nikom moved to Japan with his wife and lived there for many years before coming back to open a bakery. It's very popular and one of the best bakeries in Chiang Mai - if you ever go there, don't forget to visit Baan Bakery! Mr Boonsong Chomphusomsa met his wife when he worked in Bangkok, then they moved to Chiang Mai and opened a successful tour company called Pooh Eco Tours which offered the experience of a nature conservation trek with no elephant riding or bamboo rafting.

Some other friends who I stayed in touch with are Mr Manit Janthasing and Mr Somphot Sakarin. They both worked as trekking guides for Daret's guesthouse which organised one of the most popular treks at that time in Chiang Mai. Mr Somphot married a woman from Belgium and moved to live there with his wife for many years.

After the training programme I continued to work as a tour guide. Every morning that we wake up means that we have gained something in this life and we still have the opportunity to do what we want to with our lives. Whether in happiness or suffering, life must go on.

In late 1995, SSS guesthouse was sold to a new owner and some of us decided to move out and work elsewhere. I and my two friends, Simi Ta Por and Somchai Jai-in Otto went to work for Mr Kauw who was a former partner at SSS guesthouse. He opened a new guesthouse and jungle tour business and as we appreciated his kindness when we worked for him at SSS, we all three decided to help him by working for him in his new business.

Our new workplace was called Ploy guesthouse. It was a small building with only ten rooms located on Moonmuang Road, behind the Blue Moon night club in the city centre. When we started working there, there were only five people; three trekking guides plus the owner and a maid. The main duties were similar to what we had done at SSS. We had to get up early in the morning to pick up tourists who travelled by bus from Bangkok and use our negotiating skills to get them to stay at our guesthouse.

During this period, the trekking tour business was very competitive and this new guesthouse was small and didn't have space for many tourists. Therefore, sometimes we couldn't arrange group tours because we couldn't get enough tourists. The other problem was that we didn't have our own non-touristic trekking routes like SSS. We solved this by joining tours with other companies.

We went on various trekking routes so I got the chance to try lots of different ones, it wasn't monotonous like always doing the same route at SSS had been, but the area that stays in my mind is around the Mae Taeng river.

In that area you could find beautiful forests, waterfalls, hot spring and caves. There were many hilltribe villages scattered in the mountains such as Karen, Lahu, Lisu, Akha and Hmong and amazing hiking trails, but the most impressive part was the Mae Taeng river which many people in the area depended on for their livelihoods.

It flows from the jungle in the high mountains near the Myanmar border and is clean and large enough to do water activities like bamboo rafting, white water rafting and kayaking, but not suitable for motor-powered boats so it has the charm of a quiet river without noise from engines.

There are many rocks in the middle that cause rapids so when we did tours in this area, bamboo rafting was always thrilling and exciting, making it renowned among adventure-loving tourists.

Whenever I had chance go trekking there I enjoyed the atmosphere, staying at small bamboo hut villages on the waterside. It was fantastic and when I close my eyes and think back to thirty years ago images of this appear in my mind. Villagers made elephant and bamboo rafting camps by building bamboo huts to provide accommodation for tourists. The names of those campsites which I have never forgotten are Wang Sak, Wang Sai, Wang Von, Pang Pha Kha and Pah Ngep. (Wang means whirlpool).

The Mae Taeng river flows to meet the Ping river and at a village called Muang Kuat (Northern Thai for 'Strange Village') the river disappears into a large mountain then flows out the other side. The local people call this remarkable place Kaeng Kuat, or 'strange whirlpool'.

When I was doing jungle tours for Ploy guesthouse we had two regular routes. One of them was the southern route at Moo Baan Sop Win, Mae Wang district. In the past this beautiful area was quiet and not as busy as today. There was the small elephant camp of "Phati Daeng" (meaning Uncle Daeng) beside the river which organised elephant rides for tourists. We called this the Hmong Huai Nam Rin - Karen Huai Hoi route and the trip always started at this camp.

We then walked through the jungle to a waterfall and continued through several Karen hilltribe villages which were scattered on the high mountains in the area. It was up to the guide which village they stayed at overnight - Moo Baan Karen Huai Hoi, Moo Baan Huai Khao Liep, Moo Baan Phatu Maung, Moo Ban Khoon Puiay or Moo Baan Pha Mon - and on the last day of the trip we arrived at Moo Baan Mae Sa Pok in order to do bamboo rafting on the Mae Win river.

The other route that we offered was Pong Duad - Sob Kai which was in the Mae Taeng area. My personal favourite route was in the valley of the Mae Taeng river because bamboo rafting in this river was exciting and challenging. It was popular with many companies in Chiang Mai for this reason. Some of the main trekking companies 30 years ago included Superstar Tours, Queen Bee Tours, Daret's Tours, Chiang Mai Garden Tours, Family Tribal Tours, and Udomporn Tours and there were many others. Villagers in this area were used to seeing tourists because nearly every day they came to stay overnight in their villages.

Whenever I took tourists on a trek, I always bought bags of sweets for the village children to share. It reminded me of when I was a child and lived in a remote village - I rarely had the chance to eat sweets because there was no money and no shops to buy things like that. If the kids knew the guide named Mr Yao was coming, they would run out to welcome me because they knew on that day for sure they would have some sweets to eat. When we arrived, the children would surround us and shout "Hello! Hello! Hello!" to the foreign tourists. When the tourists said "Hello!" back, the kids would laugh and shout "Ten baht! Ten baht!" Because their English was limited, they repeated what they'd heard from their friends who had been lucky enough to get money from tourists.

The Pong Ngan village of the Lahu tribe was one of the busiest at that time because it was located near the Mae Taeng river. It was in a perfect location, about two to three hours to Moo Baan Sob Kai by bamboo raft, so lots of tour companies chose to stay there on the second night in order to do bamboo rafting to the final destination of Sob Kai on the last day. Whenever I stayed in this village I would see other trekking guides who worked for different companies.

Here's a funny story. Once, when I arrived at Pong Ngan village to stay overnight, I met an old lady I knew well because I often stayed at her house. I said "Sawadee Mea Tao" ("Hello old lady"), "Tonight I'd like to bring my tourists to stay at your house, is that okay?". She replied "No, it isn't". When I asked why not she said another guide had already booked to stay at her house. I felt a little disappointed, so I asked "Which guide? What's his name?" and she said that the guide was called 'Mr Sa Wa' ('Mr Rubbish'). "Oh no, grandma!" I said, "Don't call him Mr Rubbish!". She said his name again with a strong accent as she couldn't speak Thai well. "It really is Mr Sa Wa!" So I said I needed to see who this man was and I walked straight to her house. When I got there I couldn't stop laughing and said to myself "It's Mr Sawat who works for Queen Bee Company!" Now I understood that because her pronunciation was not clear she called him 'Mr Rubbish'! – haha!

Mr Sawat Phan Sue is another legendary guide of the Mae Taeng river route. Whenever I did the Pong Duad - Sob Kai route I always met him in the Lahu village. He had been leading tourists along this trail for a long time. There is a story about him that we laugh about among friends. When we used to do bamboo rafting, he wore trousers but no shirt in order to show off his muscular body to foreign tourists. Someone once told me that sometimes he tucked big stones into his trousers to make what was hidden underneath look majestic - haha!

As I said before, on this trekking route bamboo rafting was one of the highlights. There were many rapids along this river and every tour guide worried about possible dangers. I can say that most trekking guides experienced accidents where the bamboo raft broke apart in this river, especially during the rainy season when the water level was high. When the flow of the river was strong and fast it was harder to control the raft and sometimes it crashed onto the rocks in the middle of the river and overturned. If we couldn't push the raft off the rocks quickly it could be forced off course. It could turn in the wrong direction, get blocked by a rock or get sucked under the water. When this happened, the raft couldn't carry the weight of the passengers and their bags so we had to try to get them to the river bank as quickly as possible.

When any guide had an accident and blocked the river, other guides who were also rafting would try to park their rafts and go to the rescue. After checking that it could definitely be recovered and was still useable they would continue to their destination. If the raft was very damaged and couldn't be repaired successfully, there was only one thing to do, we had to try to find a path and walk.

Sometimes things happened which were beyond our control and what could we do when everyone's belongings were lost in the river? The main thing was to try to keep everyone safe.

I remember when I used to steer bamboo rafts. I felt it was a challenge, but I enjoyed doing it. I taught the tourists how to work as a team. We checked for stability and whether the raft was strong and working well. I made sure that it could carry weight and that there were no problems. I steered at the front and chose a helper to guide it from the back. We each carried a bamboo pole to push the raft in the direction needed with me, as captain, shouting "Left!" or "Right!". It was a lot of fun and an experience that cannot be forgotten.

During my time as a trekking guide, I was in bamboo rafting accidents many times and sometimes I was lucky to survive. There were several rapids in the Mae Taeng river that were well-known among trekking guides. They were between Moo Baan Maung Kong and Moo Baan Sob Kai and the names were Kaeng Pha Pung, Kaeng Wangsak, Kaeng Hong Kid, Kaeng Sam Sao, Kaeng Sop Thung Yua, Kaeng Wang Von, Kaeng Song Phi Nong and finally, Kaeng Sob Kai before the village of Sob Kai (Kaeng means 'rapids'). This legendary river is still there waiting for anyone who wants to experience excitement and adventure.

As for the southern route around Moo Baan Sop Win in Mae Wang district, the Huai Hoi waterfalls are one of the highlights there. The falls are not particularly big or high, but the water is clear and clean where it falls from the cliff and there is a large area for relaxing and bathing. An elderly Karen man built some bamboo huts to accommodate guides and tourists who went to stay overnight there or sometimes just stop by to dip in the water and have lunch before continuing their journey. This area was lush and green and it was very pleasant to hear water flowing down the cliff. Thinking about this place makes me happy. I often stayed overnight at the old man's bamboo campsite near the waterfall rather than in the village.

I once heard a story about one of the older legendary trekking guides from a porter who did this route with him, his name is Mr Peaw, but he calls himself John. The porter told me that once they took about ten tourists to stay at the old man's huts. After travelling through the forest and finally reaching the waterfall they were exhausted from the heat and the journey. They wanted to go down for a swim in order to cool off so they asked Mr Peaw for permission. For a joke he told them that this waterfall was a holy place for the villagers and anyone who wanted to swim there had to take off their clothes out of respect. That evening, the tourists bathed naked while Mr Paew cooked dinner on the balcony of the hut while sipping moonshine and laughing to himself!

When I had the opportunity to meet him in a pub I asked if it was a true story and he confirmed that it was. He also told me another story about a female tourist who had washed her knickers and put them to dry on a bamboo clothes line. Somehow she forgot to collect them and they stayed there. One day, Mr Paew went back with a different group of tourists and in the morning when he woke up to prepare breakfast, he saw an old Karen man dressed in the woman's knickers taking a shower in the waterfall. Mr Paew couldn't stop giggling and shouted to the old man, "Hey, where did you get those knickers?" The old man replied that someone had forgotten them a long time ago and he told himself that no-one probably wanted them back so he decided to wear them as it was a pity to waste them. Try to imagine an old man of almost seventy showering in ladies' knickers in a waterfall, it's an impressive image, haha!

During our lives, as long as we still have breath, we must continue to fight to survive. Suffering and happiness are normal elements of human life and it depends on how strong and determined our hearts are to work towards our goals. Ploy guesthouse, where we had been working, had been open for a year and finally it was the end of its time. The owner closed the business because he was unable to afford the rent and other costs.

The manager of SSS guesthouse offered us work again and we all three decided to go back there. He had plans to find a new trekking route and wanted to explore the Lisu Doi Chang - Sob Kai route which is located on the high mountains on the border of Chiang Dao and Pai district. It was an area that no tourists visited at that time.

So, one day we set off on this route and we estimated that it would take three days and two nights. There were seven of us in total; me, the guesthouse owner, my two friends Mr Sinchai To-a and Mr Somchai Jai-in and some local men who knew the area very well.

On the first day, it took more than four hours by car to pass through Huai Nam National Park which was a popular place to see the 'sea of fog'. We continued driving up a high mountain to a destination called Doi Chang from where it was possible to see as far as the city of Pai. Then we walked into the forest, which felt terrifyingly dense to me and hiked up several hills to reach Moo Baan Lisu Doi Chang village. We worked out that it took about four hours on foot to arrive at the village on our first day.

In the Lisu Doi Chang village lived about twenty families surrounded by mountain forests. We were greeted by the village head man and after negotiations they allowed us to bring tourists to stay in the village in the future.

On the second day before leaving the village for our next destination, the local man who was leading us on this trip told us that we had to walk up and down through the jungle for six to seven hours that day. The plan was to go to the elephant and bamboo rafting campsite in the middle of the jungle next to the Mae Taeng river. We stayed overnight at the campsite of a Karen man named Phati Padi (Uncle Padi).

In this programme there was no hiking on the last day. Instead we planned to offer elephant riding and bamboo rafting on the Mae Taeng river because the hiking on the first and second days was quite strenuous. Bamboo rafting from the campsite to Moo Baan Sob Kai took at least six to seven hours. This route was quite difficult in my opinion, but when we got back we agreed that we would offer it to tourists in the future. Reunited again at SSS guesthouse, my friends and I would start a new trekking route which everyone agreed was very challenging and difficult.

It's hard to predict what the future holds, but the thing to remember is not to give up. For me, what happened in the past is a valuable experience. As a trekking guide I discovered my strengths and weaknesses and I was happy that many trekking companies and guesthouses were ready to give me the opportunity to work for them.

I would like to encourage all readers, no matter what you are thinking of doing, to keep moving forward. Don't stop, overcome the big and small obstacles. If you have a passion or a dream, hurry to pursue it, don't give up, don't let time pass and regret it later. Determination and good principles will lead you towards that dream. No matter how many times you fall, get up and keep fighting and treat your problems and mistakes as lessons. Fix them then carry on. There are no losers and no one wins forever. As long as we are alive, we must fight to the end.

Life must go on!

The Trekking Guide ชีวิตข้าไกด์ทัวร์ป่า

Chapter 11 - Life is Like a River

Around the year 1994, I took tourists on a trek around Doi Chang near the Pai district. The Lisu Doi Chang route was very tough during the winter because the weather on the high mountains is especially cold. If anybody reading this book has travelled in the high land around Huai Nam Dang National Park in winter, you will have seen the phenomenon known as the 'sea of mist'.

Sometimes visibility is bad due to the mist and you can't see the road or the area around you clearly. On a day with good visibility and clear weather, you can see a very beautiful sea of mist. The clouds in the sky look like waves, creating a very special atmosphere.

I remember when I took tourists there for the first time. We stayed in a Lisu family's hut and during the night we had just a thin blanket and a pillow. It was so cold, but fortunately for me in every hilltribe village you will find some kind of local homemade liquor and before going to sleep I drank the Lisu tribe's corn liquor to warm my body.

On the second evening, at the bamboo raft campsite in the forest beside the river, we lit a big fire to stay warm. The next day we had to leave as early as possible to arrive at our destination on time because rafting along this route took five to six hours. It was freezing cold in the early morning.

During the dry season, the water in the river is very low and we were often delayed on the rafts because of the exposed rocks. Sometimes it was very difficult to get past these rocks and it took time to pull, drag and lift the raft when it got stuck. My friend, Niran Muangkham (Mr T), once had to use a torch to see the way while rafting because he was unable to reach his destination before dusk. It is extremely dangerous rafting at night because mistakes can happen at any time and in the darkness you cannot clearly see the river ahead.

During the wintertime it gets dark more quickly, especially when hiking in the jungle where there are large trees on both sides of the trail that block the sunlight, so this route was difficult in many ways. We had to be careful and the tourists had to be prepared for a challenge.

In the rainy season, it was extra difficult on some parts of this trekking route. We walked through rainforest where blood-sucking leeches lived on the wet ground and on the leaves on both sides of the path. We had to encourage tourists not to be afraid or panic about this. We tried to explain that leeches can bite and suck blood, but in general they are not dangerous even if they can cause a little pain and itching. However, you can imagine when anyone from a city is faced with a horde of blood sucking leeches in the jungle, they will be frightened!

We warned tourists that if they were itchy or felt something on their body, they should check it out immediately. If you brush past leeches they might cling to your shoes and get inside your clothes and tourists often liked to wear shorts and t-shirts, they were easy targets.

On almost every trip along this route during the rainy season I heard tourists shouting for help because a leech had jumped into their shoes and gone inside their shirt or trousers without them noticing. When someone realised there was something strange inside their clothes they had to take them off to check. It could be awkward when it was a female tourist who was screaming with fear and the guide had to remove the leech!

Later, I was advised by the villagers to take salt or ashes with me as a leech which has either of these sprinkled on it will die instantly. This solution is a good example of the valuable knowledge of the local people of the forest.

During the rainy season the ground became wet and muddy and you could easily slip and fall. There were feelings of exhaustion, tears and sometimes amusement when travelling companions fell over on the slippery trails. We had to help each other up or carry luggage for someone who was weaker. This supportive atmosphere created a feeling of empathy between us, and even though we were only together for a short period of time, sometimes people grew close to each other.

I don't know why, but I had a feeling of fear about the Doi Chang route. I was afraid of being robbed along the way. Maybe it was just my imagination because there weren't many people or villages, making it difficult to contact someone for help if something happened.

There were stories of drug smuggling in the area which made me worry every time I took tourists there, but fortunately, in nearly thirty years of being a trekking guide, I never experienced any robberies. However, guide Mr Pinit Ithaban and three or four other guides were robbed while rafting on the Mae Taeng river. Mr Charan Nantarak (guide Bob) told me the story in an amusing way. He said that the robbery was committed by some hilltribe people - the guides knew this from the way they spoke. They had a funny accent and the Thai guides had to try not to laugh. The exchange was comical because the thieves spoke Thai badly and their pronunciation wasn't clear (hilltribe languages and Thai are completely different). In the end no one was harmed as the thieves were only interested in valuables. It was a bad situation, but it ended with everyone safe and the trekking guides had a funny tale to tell their fellow guides back in Chiang Mai.

The life can be risky depending on your luck. There are so many responsibilities on each trip and it's difficult to predict what will happen. It was said that people doing this job would either end up as alcoholics or drug addicts. It wasn't always certain who would have the discipline and determination not to be tempted by these things. It was fun spending time with foreigners who were there to have a good time and learn new things, and entertainment often involved parties so it was easy for drinking to become a habit. It all depends on how you behave - poison doesn't harm you if you don't touch it, but it can if you eat or drink it carelessly.

Some guides I knew well married foreign women and left that lifestyle to begin new lives abroad, for example, guide Suchat

The Trekking Guide ชีวิตข้าไกด์ทัวร์ป่า

Yodkhiri Phao Phrai married a Canadian woman, moved to Canada to pursue his dream of running a Muay Thai boxing business and has become well-known all over the world. Guide Threerayut Tham Wong also married a Canadian woman, moved to live with his wife, finished his education and still lives in Canada now. Two other trekking guides, Mr Nish Inthabun and Mr Pan Sae Sue married English women and moved to the UK where Mr Nish owns a Thai restaurant. Mr Pan Sae Sue, after living in the UK for a few years, moved to Auckland in New Zealand where he works as a head chef in a restaurant.

There are many other trekking guides that I haven't mentioned who married foreigners and now live all over the world. It gave me hope that someday I would have the opportunity to visit a foreign country, but in our lives we can't assume anything will happen. Sometimes we do everything we can to get what we hope for and don't succeed. Instead we get things that we don't expect and don't necessarily want.

There is a saying that certainty and uncertainty always come together and if we don't expect too much, we won't be disappointed. We have to understand that emotions, both good and bad, will come and go so we must recognise them for what they really are and know how to let go of them. If not, they will harm us. Emotions are fleeting and sometimes just one moment of bad temper can ruin a person's life. Feelings of both happiness and suffering appear and disappear all the time. If we don't have awareness of this and know how to let go of them it can lead to disaster. Bad things can happen when people do something suddenly without thinking because of their feelings or thoughts in that moment.

Our life is like a river that, once it has flowed past, cannot flow back again. Quite often while trekking on the Lisu Doi Chang route, I stayed overnight in a bamboo hut in a peaceful forest near the river. I used to sit and watch as the river flowed, letting my thoughts flow with it and wondering where they would end up. Both time and water, once they have flowed, cannot go back to where they were. In the same way our lives which are constantly flowing forward leave everything in the past. All that's left are memories that are deeply ingrained in our minds. Memories of the past sometimes bring happiness and sometimes cause suffering, it depends on what we choose to remember. Events of the past should be taken as lessons.

When I think back to myself as a child born into a poor family, I never imagined that I would experience so many things to be remembered. I had the chance to do a job I loved, travelling through the forest to hundreds of villages in Northern Thailand. I had the good fortune to meet a lot of people, both from hilltribes and tourists from all over the world. I've travelled to many places that people dream of visiting thanks to my work as a guide and sometimes by backpacking by myself. I've had a lot of fun doing what I enjoyed and learning new things through experiences. Everything I did in my life as a trekking guide will always remain in my memory.

I never had a bad situation that led to a serious accident involving a tourist. There was, however, one incident where I was lucky not to be badly injured. I was taking a group of Canadian tourists to the Huai Nam Dang area. There were four students from Payap University who came to work as apprentices and one porter who was my brother. The incident happened on the second day when we were staying overnight at a Karen village. I had asked to stay with a villager who had built a hut on a high bank near the river. After dinner, we all sat in a circle on the balcony of the hut which had no railings. We were chatting and sipping on the villagers' moonshine whiskey when I got up to go to the toilet. As I stood up, I fell from the balcony and rolled down a steep bank of bamboo towards the river. I lost consciousness and don't remember anything after that. The next day, someone told me that the villagers had made a bamboo torch to find me and they had brought me up from the bottom of the hill.

Another incident that I remember well was in the Mae Wang area. On that trip, there were eleven tourists of various nationalities. Along the way, in the middle of the forest, there were large vines hanging from tall trees. It was the perfect place to swing out over the edge of the cliff. I think many guides who passed along this route stopped to swing like Tarzan. One time, as I swung on the vine to show off to the tourists some of them asked if they could have a go. I said okay, but warned them that they had to be careful because if something went wrong, I couldn't take responsibility. A few people tried it and everyone seemed to enjoy it. Then it was the turn of a Swedish woman. She grabbed the rope and swung over the cliff but, for some unknown reason, before swinging back she let go of it and fell to the ground far below.

In a panic, myself, a porter and another tourist rushed down to help her. We found her and provided first aid and were able to bring her up safely. She was shocked by the incident and while both of her legs were fine, her right arm was injured. We helped her to Moo Baan Huai Hoi, a Karen village, where fortunately there was a school teacher who had a pickup truck. I sent the tourist with the teacher for hospital treatment in Chiang Mai. I was very lucky that she wasn't seriously harmed.

There was a tragic incident that happened to a friend of mine. He was leading a trek in the Mae Taeng area and had to take his tourists across a river to reach the village on the other side. As everyone was crossing the river, one of the women suddenly got swept away by the current. It happened so fast that nobody could help her in time.

My friend was heartbroken. Even though it wasn't his fault, as the guide who took the tourists to that place he felt responsible and it hurt him deeply. He decided to become a monk for some time so that he could release the woman's soul according to Buddhist belief.

No matter how careful we are, if something is going to happen it can happen at any time. When it's our time to die, nothing can stop that, we can't choose our destiny and we can't escape our fate.

Between 1997 and 2007 there was a lot of competition in the jungle tour industry and some guesthouses had to close down because they couldn't afford the rising costs. At the same time the number of visitors to Thailand started to fall as Laos, Cambodia, Myanmar and Vietnam opened up to tourists.

SSS guesthouse was sold to new owners so, like bees breaking away from their hive, my friends and I scattered in different directions, looking for new places to work. Goodbye SSS guesthouse, I will remember you fondly forever. I felt sad and missed the good old days of working with my friends. I thought of our many adventures together, the happy and sad times we shared and the songs that we sang together when partying at the guesthouse, laughing, quarrelling, arguing, teasing and supporting each other.

All these memories are like a river that has flowed past and cannot flow back again. Just like time passes through the night to the next day, tomorrow becomes the past and eventually disappears. In the end, only memories remain and it is up to us whether we choose to hold on to them or let them disappear to be replaced by the new things that happen every day. Nothing can stop time.

Life is like a river!

Chapter 12 - Life is an Illusion

Ajahn Buddhadasa Bhikku, a Thai master monk, said we shouldn't take life too seriously because it isn't real. Life doesn't actually exist, it is simply a series of events that appear, settle then disappear. In the end we have to return everything to nature. Even the body that we cherish and care for every day, when the time comes, that too goes back to nature. Don't mourn the past, don't worry about the future, just do your best in the present. This is enough to not make your heart suffer.

After SSS guesthouse closed, I was contacted about a job at a new guesthouse called Chanchai. I decided to apply immediately and was warmly welcomed there. The owners, Mr Roon and Ms Tong, were very kind and friendly.

It's a small world. At this guesthouse I met a friend who I had worked with at SSS, Niranan Muangkham (Mr T). I also met other guides who were already working there, Mr Sunthorn Yaniwong, Mr Chairat Rincome ('Ninja') and his wife Miss Noi and Mr Jane Kham Lai ('Junny'). Altogether there were six of us happily working together like a family.

I thought of my youngest brother, Suchart Sripuri, who lived with my parents in the village and had no opportunity to study. The owner of the guesthouse kindly gave me permission to bring him to work as a porter as I wanted to help him learn languages from tourists. I thought this might be one way that could lead him towards a better future and I brought him to live with me in a small rented room near our work. It didn't take long for him to pick up some English thanks to the help of the other guides there.

The trekking route that we offered was a southern route called Kariang Huai Tong - Mae Na Jon. It was a three-day two-night itinerary where we didn't meet other tourist groups and it was slightly different from the original route of SSS guesthouse that I used to do. We travelled south of Chiangmai through San Pa Tong and Mae Wang districts then hiked into the forest and mountains which are adjacent to the border of Doi Inthanon National Park.

The highlight of this route was the beautiful Doi Inthanon, the highest mountain in Thailand. There we visited Phra Mahathat Naphamethanidon and Phra Mahathat Bhumiponsiri, the twin pagodas which the Royal Thai Air Force built as an offering to His Majesty King Bhumibol Adulyadej and Queen Sirikit. We also visited Wachirathan waterfall, one of the largest and most beautiful waterfalls in Chiang Mai. This route was a lot easier than the Lisu Doi Chang route, but at the same time both routes had their own charms due to their distinct geological features.

The daily routine at Chanchai guesthouse was no different from SSS guesthouse. I had to wake up early in the morning to wait for the tourist buses and offer accommodation at our guesthouse. We also provided tourist information and tried to sell trekking tours. Sometimes I got fed up with waking up early to pick up tourists, especially because I had to talk to them about staying at our guesthouse when in some cases they had already made plans to stay elsewhere. We had to try to make them change their minds and stay with us, which I thought was unfair to them. Maybe it was because I had been doing this for quite some time, but I felt awkward in these situations.

During my time at Chanchai guesthouse, I often got into trouble for waking up late. The rule was that anyone who overslept and couldn't pick up tourists lost their place in the queue for work, otherwise it wasn't fair for the other guides who had got up on time. I got punished like this on a regular basis when I was working there. As I was the only single man while all the other guides were married and had families, I often had the opportunity to take foreign girls out to drink in bars at night and then I woke up late with a hangover and couldn't go to work.

Despite this I think working there was one of the best times of my career as a trekking guide. Looking back on those days always makes me smile. In the evening, if Mr T and I didn't have a tour we would play the guitar and sing with the foreigners staying at the guesthouse. Sometimes the wives of the married guides would come and yell at them to come home – it was hilarious!

I felt safer hiking on this route than on the Lisu Doi Chang route because there was no border with Myanmar. The area had many villages scattered around and sometimes we passed villagers on their way to work in the fields. Also, on the Mae Chaem river there were no dangerous rapids like on the Mae Tang river so I was less worried about many things on this route.

The area was difficult for cars during the rainy season. The roads were narrow and there were dangerous spots on cliff edges. As it was a dirt road, when it rained it became muddy and slippery. Sometimes our car got stuck and couldn't take us to our destination. When this happened, us guides had to have a backup plan to get the tourists there. This meant we had to walk for twice as long and maybe spend the night in huts that the Hmong and Karen tribes had built as shelters for when they worked on the land. They were very basic, but they had some cooking equipment that we could use to prepare food. In such cases we had to explain the reason for the change of plan to our tourists and sometimes it turned out that they enjoyed it more than the original plan. Usually they were polite and patient and accepted the situation in good spirits.

The village that we went to if the tour included elephant riding was Moo Baan Mae Na Jon Noi belonging to the Karen tribe. This village sits high on a mountain with beautiful panoramic views. The Karen people have the skills to catch and train wild elephants which have been passed down from their ancestors. Before tourism, villagers used elephants for work such as hauling logs and transportation. Any villager who owned an elephant was regarded as having a good status.

We stayed at the Hmong Khoon Mae Wak village on the first night as long as nothing happened that caused a change of plan. It was a large village with twenty families, not too far from Mae Na Jon Noi where we stopped for lunch and elephant riding. After that we went to a waterfall to freshen up before continuing to Moo Baan

Mai Karen village for the second night. On the third day we travelled to Uncle Saen's bamboo rafting camp beside the Mae Jam River where we took bamboo rafts to Moo Baan Mae Na Jon village, had lunch and waited for our car to pick us up.

    Every time I stayed overnight at a hilltribe village I enjoyed the peaceful atmosphere without electricity or annoying traffic noises. I remember those days in the small bamboo huts of the elders from the Hmong and Karen tribes. We would sit around drinking local moonshine whisky and smoking opium with the old men. Sometimes, on a journey to learn new things, people want to try something they've never done before and some of my tourists wanted to try smoking opium. I have fond memories of sitting in a circle with foreign tourists taking turns to smoke opium. It was an experience of a lifetime that I won't forget.

    One day at the guesthouse I met a young woman from Australia who had done a trekking tour with guide Sunthorn Yaniwong. After her trip she decided to stay. We had good conversations and got to know each other very well. I took her to various places in Chiang Mai and Chiang Rai as well as to my parents' house. She was beautiful and very kind and one of the nicest women I have ever met. We spent several weeks together until she had to leave.

    We both promised that we would stay in touch and if we were lucky, we would meet again. In all the time that I had been a trekking guide, she was the first woman that I ever thought about when we were apart. Her aim was to travel to other countries to experience life and on the day we said goodbye, she promised that she would come back. It was a test of my own mind how long I could believe that and wait for her return.

    Time is constantly moving forward. With every day that passes, something new comes along to replace what happened before. Everything changes with time - objects, buildings, even our own minds. As for the Australian woman and I, we kept in touch by letter and occasionally by phone, which was not so easy with the lack of technology back then. We continued to communicate for some time until eventually things went quiet on her side and I wasn't sure I would ever get the chance to see her again.

I carried on with my life at the guesthouse until one day we all received bad news from the owner that it was closing. It was a nightmare for all of us to find a new job. Daily life can change for different reasons, just like with Chanchai guesthouse. Once we spent our days working together happily, but then it was time for a change. We have to accept whatever happens and be prepared to face it. Goodbye Chanchai guesthouse, you will always be in my heart.

The events that happen in our lives are just a series of changes – nothing is permanent. They are illusions that we can't hold onto because everything moves on, everything is temporary. There are many dimensions to our lives. We shouldn't try to hold onto something that makes us unable to change or accept that new things may happen. For example, there may be someone that you think loves you very much, but then one day they break up with you because they love someone else. That is not necessarily wrong - they may have been in love with you before, but aren't anymore. It's like if you used to enjoy eating a certain kind of food, but then one day you decide that it's no longer tasty even though it's the same food. So don't listen to your thoughts too much because everything is uncertain.

In this world of uncertainty, we are caught in a social trap that stipulates that we must follow certain rules and place importance on material possessions and the person who has the most is the winner. But in fact, nothing really belongs to us. Everything must be returned to nature, even our own lives. We must accept that we will have to let things go, otherwise suffering will be in our hearts forever.

When we look back, there are many people that we used to know and live with such as parents, siblings, grandparents, relatives and close friends, but then one day they die and we never see them again. Have we ever wondered where they all disappeared to? And for ourselves, when it's time to leave this world, do we have an answer yet about where we are going to go?

If you ask yourself what exactly you want in life, often the answer is to work to support your family. But at the same time, the rules of society that divide us into rich and poor make us selfish.

People work hard and compete for their own wealth and power, even doing bad things sometimes. When we obtain these things, we may be happy for a short time, but when death comes we can't take them with us. Remember that we know the day we are born, but we cannot know the day we will die. We need to slow down and think about what exactly we are living for.

 I thanked the owner of the guesthouse for giving me the opportunity to work there for many years and said goodbye. I walked out with a heavy and confused heart, not knowing my destination. I found a small room to rent in Chiang Mai in Moon Muang Road Soi 9 in a building belonging to Ms Aree Sunyaluck, who I knew well and respected like a sister. She had opened a shop to teach traditional Thai massage to tourists. I didn't feel so lonely there because I met new people who came to study almost every day.

 I sat and thought about which direction to go in order to make a living. A voice in my head and heart told me that I still loved my career as a trekking guide. It was a life of freedom - living alone, having food and a little money to spend every day was enough for me. During that time I was working on a freelance basis, so companies or guesthouses hired me to go trekking and I said yes to every route they offered me. It was difficult as I didn't have regular work like I did with the guesthouses, but I was determined and ready to face anything that might happen in the future because I was doing what I loved.

 Every day I would drive my motorcycle to tour offices and guesthouses running treks to ask if there were any jobs available. I had the opportunity to go on many trekking routes such as Phrao - Chiang Dao, Muang Kong - Sob Kai, Lisu Mae Ja and so many others that I can't name them all.

 Happiness and suffering are just illusions floating in the air like dreams that have passed by and gone. There is no point thinking about the past or worrying about what is yet to come. Just think good, do good, and do your best for today - that's enough.

Life is an illusion!

The Trekking Guide ชีวิตข้าไกด์ทัวร์ป่า

Chapter 13 - Life is Letting Go

The world can be a beautiful and peaceful place if people are kind. When we are born into this world we need to give love, generosity, care and understanding to each other. It all starts with our parents, without whom we would not exist. They raise us and take care of us from the moment we are born. They give us the great gift of unconditional love without expecting anything in return.

Giving from one human being to another is essential for us all to be able to live together in peace. If we all know how to give love and compassion, to share, sacrifice and forgive, our world will be a better place. Giving is a more noble and joyful act than receiving, to give is better than to get. Greed and desire cause chaos and destroy peace. Our lives are full of expectation and the struggle to obtain everything that our hearts desire.

Often, when we get something we want, it makes us happy temporarily but then we want the next thing. This happens over and over again. If we don't get what we want or expect we suffer and for some people life can become miserable. If you want to avoid suffering, don't expect too much and try to change from being a receiver to being a giver instead.

My life as a trekking guide changed my destiny in many ways and my experience of working for many different guesthouses taught me that nothing is permanent. I am lucky that I am someone who doesn't think too hard about life. If something needs to be done, I just do it the best I can. I don't worry too much about the future as it may prevent me from being able to enjoy the present. Maybe because I am a person who has never thought too big, with no clear goal in life such as becoming a millionaire, my life is simple.

There is no framework or clear path for life. After leaving Chanchai guesthouse to rent a room alone and work as a freelance guide, my routine was to drive my motorcycle to see Payap Ariya, an old friend who had opened a tour office on Thaphae Road. I helped him by giving information to travellers who were interested in going on a jungle tour and if we got enough people, I was able to be their guide. I also visited Daret's guesthouse regularly because I had many friends who worked there. I would go there to eat, drink and advise tourists about tours alongside my fellow guides in the hope of getting work.

Daret's guesthouse was one of the most well-known places for tourist accommodation and trekking trips in those days. Travellers used to eat and drink there every day because of the atmosphere and the spacious communal area at the front overlooking the moat near Thaphae Gate. It was considered as one of the best locations in Chiang Mai at that time and many trekking guides began their training there.

I have many friends that I am still quite close to and I would like to name some of them. Soonthron Phu Nak Kiaow was a young man with long hair from the northeast who everyone called Mr Bank. He was a legendary trekking guide with lots of funny stories to tell. Bua Lai Chom Mala or as we called him, guide Hod, was the man who could drink a lot of moonshine, but never got drunk. Another one is Manit Juntasing from Petchaboon, a friend I was with for a long time when I was working as a freelance guide. Each trekking guide has so many funny and interesting stories that it's impossible to tell them all in this book.

Most trekking guides came from poor families and were ordained as monks and lived in temples so that they could get an education. There are many from the northeast and some from hilltribe families who started off as porters. We all had to fight to gain knowledge in order to live a better life. Therefore, being a fighter who endures hardships in life is in the blood of every trekking guide.

Another guesthouse that I worked for was Your House guesthouse. The owner was Mrs Sin who had a French husband and most of her customers were French. Maybe because he was good at marketing, a lot of tourists stayed there and I often had the opportunity to work for them. Their main trekking route was the Lisu Mae Ja route, located to the north of Chiang Mai.

At this guesthouse I met a new friend. His name was Chaiyong Techahongsa or, as tourists called him, guide Fang. He was a cool young man from Lampang who was passionate about western music and left a lot of western women with broken hearts! He rented a room near mine on Moon Muang Road Soi 9 and we helped each other out during difficult times when there wasn't much work.

On the Lisu Mae Ja route we travelled north from Chiang Mai and passed through the district of Chiang Dao. At a large road junction we had to turn left to go through Muang Ngai sub-district towards Wiang Haeng district. If you went straight on at the junction along the main road you would pass through the districts of Fang and reach the border at Baan Tha Ton in Mae Ai district.

On this route, there were mountains stretching almost to the Thai-Myanmar border. The journey to the start of the route at Moo Baan Lisu Mae Ja village took about three hours by car. The main road was quite easy, but it was difficult when we turned off to go to the village because it was a dirt road so dusty in the summer and wet and muddy in the rainy season.

In this region there are people from various hilltribes such as Shan, Karen, Lahu and Lisu because it borders Myanmar. Further towards the border crossing in Wiang Haeng district there are a lot of Shan and Karen people in particular. Many of them secretly cross the border from Myanmar to escape clashes between military forces over land that they owned before it was put under the rule of the Myanmar government. The resistance of the Shan and Karen ethnic minorities fighting for their liberation from Myanmar junta rule leads to regular clashes.

When I went to Lisu Mae Ja for the first time, I stood and looked at the forest and mountains that stretched as far as the eye could see and wondered who was brave enough to live in that wilderness. This trekking route passed through Lisu, Lahu and

Karen villages. I was assured by the villagers that this area was peaceful and without any danger.

After I had been on that route a few times I became impressed by how kind and helpful the villagers were and by their simple way of life in the forest. This three-day two-night route was not as difficult as many areas that I had been to. On the first day, it took only two hours from Lisu Mae Ja village to Moo Baan Lahu Mae village and on the second day, we walked along the villagers' trail for about three hours through the forest to a waterfall where we stopped for lunch. Here, an old man named Jafoo from a Lahu village had built some bamboo huts for tourists to use as shelters. Each guide who passed that way paid the old man a small fee to use his huts and he brought snacks and drinks to sell in order to earn a little money.

After swimming in the waterfall we continued our journey to the elephant camp which belonged to a Karen man, Pha Ti Tong, who had built a few bamboo huts for the mahouts and tourists. From there we travelled by elephant to Moo Baan Mae Kon Nai, a Karen hilltribe village, where we stayed for the second night. On the last day, we walked for two hours through Shan and Lisu villages to the Ping river for bamboo rafting then we stopped for lunch in a small shop beside the road where the car came to pick us up.

The Lisu Mae Ja area is another place which is hard to forget because of the memories that were created there. I met people who had a hard life, living in small bamboo huts without any home comforts, not even electricity. They worked in difficult conditions in the hot sun all day. Once their work was finished, they came home, ate just enough food to survive and had no entertainment for relaxing.

Every time I took tourists there and saw how they lived, I imagined that it was a life without happiness, but who am I to judge or criticize? They may not have had big and beautiful houses or luxurious food or vehicles like people in the city, but maybe they were happier than city people who had all the modern conveniences yet were not happy at all. There are many stories about rich people who have everything and are still not satisfied, but whenever I went to stay in the villagers' bamboo huts, I noticed that they seemed to be smiling and kind even though they didn't have any possessions.

I still remember how every time our car arrived at the Lisu Mae Ja village where we started our trek, there was an old man and a young man in the village who asked to join the trip as porters in exchange for a wage to support their families. Sometimes I had to witness the disappointed face of someone I had to refuse - I couldn't hire many porters each time because it cost too much. But I had a rule that if one time I hired an old man, the next time I would hire a young man instead to maintain a good relationship between us.

Among all the porters who worked with me there was often an old man named Bobo and a young man named Yut. Every time we finished a trek and I paid them for their work they had such a big smile on their faces, it made me so happy.

I continued to live my life as a freelance guide and led tourists on many trekking routes for almost two years. Guide Fang was fortunate enough to meet a young French woman. They fell in love and had a son and he decided to move to France to start a new life there. He and I didn't communicate for a while, but later I heard the news that he had returned from France, so we met and worked together again.

We had the opportunity to work for a new guesthouse called Nice Place. The owner offered anyone who brought tourists to stay a commission, so many taxi and tuktuk drivers took their passengers there.

The owner had contacts at various tour operators in Bangkok's Khao San Road and arranged a special overnight bus to Chiang Mai specifically for backpackers. This brought many people to stay at his guesthouse and book treks. So, every morning those who worked there had to wake up early to pick up tourists arriving from Bangkok and bring them back to the guesthouse just like in many of the other places where I had worked. Nice Place was very busy with tours so at that time many trekking guides of all ages worked there and it was a lot of fun.

While there I met a young woman from America and we were together for several years. Maybe destiny brought us together? In

Buddhism, we believe in reincarnation and that in a previous life we may have been friends, partners, family or even enemies and it is not a coincidence that in this life we may meet again in different forms.

One day while I was on duty, a taxi driver brought a young female tourist to help her find a place to stay. After talking for a bit I learned that she had been teaching English in Japan and after her contract there had ended she wanted to visit Thailand before returning to America. I could speak some Japanese which impressed her. I asked her which state she lived in and she said Michigan. I told her that I had a friend named Joe who lived there as well. A few years ago I had taken him on a trek while I was working at Chanchai guesthouse. He gave me his address and invited me to visit him in Michigan someday if I had the opportunity. I showed her Joe's address and she looked shocked and exclaimed how incredible it was. It was such a coincidence, she knew Joe very well because they had attended the same university in Michigan.

After that, negotiating was easy and friendly and she agreed to stay at the guesthouse and go on a trek with me. The next day, I led 12 tourists, including her, on a three-day two-night trip in the Mae Wang district, south of Chiang Mai and we got to know each other better. Afterwards I took the group for a drink at the Riverside bar. Everyone talked about the trip and what a wonderful time they'd had together and then said their goodbyes.

I asked the American girl what she wanted to do next and she said that she wanted to study Thai massage and asked me to help her find a place to study. It seemed that destiny was on my side. It was very easy to find a place for her to study because the room I lived in was next to a Thai massage school where my friend was the teacher, so I took her there to enrol on the course. We spent more time together and after the course she got a job as a teacher at an international school in Chiang Mai.

My life during this period was filled with happiness and hope for a future married life. We agreed to move in together to a new apartment which was luxurious for a jungle tour guide like me. However, fate played a trick on me while I was happily living with my American girlfriend. The young woman from Australia who I had dated and who had promised to return came back. It was very awkward for me because I hadn't expected her to come back as we had been out of touch for so long. It was a pity, both girls were very good and sincere people who had shown me love and kindness.

In the end, I chose to stay with the American woman, but I thought about the pain of the other woman who was so disappointed. Was I a selfish person who caused a good woman to suffer for my actions? I was such a coward that I didn't even dare to apologize to her at that time, it was something that I was embarrassed about. I prayed for good luck for her and forgiveness for hurting her kind heart. I can only think that sometimes we can't force destiny. Life stories are hard to predict, happiness and sadness don't exist, they're just transitional emotions. If our hearts do not know how to let go, we will suffer. Indeed, everyone gets separated in the end.

My relationship with the American woman was going well. If I wasn't on a trekking tour, I would pick her up by motorcycle from the school where she worked. We travelled together to many places and were happy together. One day she told me the good news that she would like to take me to America to introduce me to her parents, relatives and friends. I was so excited to visit America for the first time. I never expected that I would have the opportunity to visit one of the world's most modern countries.

When I applied for a visa at the consulate in Chiang Mai, I had no confidence that it would be granted because everyone knew that for Thai people it was very difficult to be allowed into America. I waited for an answer and eventually received the news that I had permission to go as a tourist for three months. I was very excited to travel abroad as I used to dream that once in my life I would do it.

Everything went smoothly thanks to my girlfriend. After getting my visa, we began to prepare the trip. She planned to leave earlier to prepare things at her parents' house and then I had to travel alone to meet her there. The long-awaited day finally arrived and I remember well the nerves about everything that could go wrong. I had some experience of short flights, but this time I had to travel across the sea for thousands of miles. I was nervous and curious at the same time.

I flew with Eva air, Taiwan's national airline. The journey was quite long, taking almost two days from Bangkok to Taipei, from Taipei to Los Angeles, from Los Angeles to Chicago and from Chicago to Michigan. It was quite difficult to travel alone for the first time, especially with multiple plane transfers and a long waiting time between each flight. Sometimes I would be worried that I'd get lost because this wasn't the jungle, it was a foreign country where people didn't speak Thai! Thanks to my experience as a tour guide and being familiar with foreigners, I had enough confidence to ask for information if I was unsure, and I finally made it to Michigan safely.

I could hardly believe that I had the chance to go to America. A poor jungle boy had arrived in this land that many people dream of visiting once in their lifetime. It was beyond the expectations of a trekking guide like me. My girlfriend took me to visit many famous places, giving me the opportunity to learn about the western way of life. It is such a good memory. I am deeply grateful to her for taking such great care of me and to all her family, relatives and friends for their warm welcome. It was a great feeling to be able to travel and to see and do new things in a foreign country which were completely different from the way I lived in Thailand.

After we came back from the United States, everything went back to normal and I returned to work at Nice Place guesthouse. However, it became more difficult for me because I was used to living a free life because I had always been alone. Now there was another person to consider, but I was addicted to the fun of working as a trekking guide, drinking with friends and returning home late at night, causing me and my girlfriend to argue with each other.

When I thought about the past while I was writing this book I realised that at that time I'd had the opportunity to do something new for myself, but I never considered doing it. My girlfriend suggested many new things to do, but I had no serious interest in any of them.

Sometimes we can't understand our own actions. Even if we have the chance to do other things, we don't do them. During the time that she and I lived together as a couple, I still lived my life as a free-spirited trekking guide without thinking of finding another career with better prospects. My actions were the same every day and she became annoyed with this.

I consider myself lucky to have known her. She was always kind, patient and forgiving of my actions. We had the opportunity to travel around Southeast Asia to Indonesia, Bali, Vietnam, Laos and Cambodia while we were together. It was a happy time for me, visiting many countries and, without her, I wouldn't have been able to do it.

Then one day there was an economic downturn in Thailand, we called it the Tom Yum Goong crisis. The currency weakened and was unlikely to recover quickly. This event had a huge impact on my girlfriend because she received a Thai salary and when it was exchanged for dollars it had almost no value. For this reason, she decided to go back to America to study for a Master's degree. I understood the reason and agreed because it was her life and she had to do what was best for her.

After she left she emailed me to tell me that she had found a place to study and invited me to go to America to live with her and find a way to make a living there. I was very happy and excited to have the opportunity to go back once again to make a new life there. I prepared my visa and other documents and it was not long before my second trip to America.

We rented a small flat in Ann Arbor city near the University of Michigan where she was studying. I started my new life there by just doing the housework and cooking. It wasn't easy to change my whole way of life. In this quiet little university city I wanted to get a job, but it was impossible because my visa didn't allow me to work. My life was quite lonely, I didn't have friends and the culture was so different to mine. As a trekking guide who enjoyed a simple life it was quite stressful for me. I checked to see if there was a Thai association or if there were any Thai restaurants around but there were none.

My dreams and goals for a new life weren't as beautiful as I'd imagined, everything seemed dark to me. My thoughts became chaotic, I was tired of being there and yearned for the free life of a trekking guide. I was quite confused about what to do. Although I was with a woman I loved, the other side of my mind wasn't happy. My girlfriend saw that and suggested that I continue my studies if I wanted to and she would support me financially, but I didn't accept her offer.

I began to think of myself as a weak person and I lost my self-confidence. I woke up every day with no enthusiasm, not knowing how to live in the American system, so one day she said that if I wanted to return to Thailand, when she graduated we could decide how to move forward with our lives. I was very disappointed in myself. She gave me many opportunities, but I couldn't do any better, I still couldn't find my own purpose in life. I decided to go back to Thailand even though I still had time remaining on my visa, leaving her to study there alone.

I went back to working as a trekking guide again. Being able to go back and do what I was good at and have freedom made me relax a little, but life is strange. Sometimes it's complicated and it's hard to understand what true happiness is. When I went back to doing what I loved I felt happier, but deep down I worried about my girlfriend. It was a loneliness that could not be explained and every day I looked forward to seeing her again soon.

I heard that many of my trekking guide friends had married and gone to live abroad with their wives including guide Eak Daret who moved to England, guide Chailek who moved to America, guide Leam who went to Sweden, guide Pid who moved to Belgium, guide Cha Muangkong who went to Denmark and guide Nikom Tanawa who was in Japan. It secretly made me sad that it hadn't worked out for me when I'd had the opportunity to live abroad.

My girlfriend and I kept in touch by e-mail. Our relationship was still good, but I was worried that our love would end without us meeting again. Every day I looked forward to the time when she would graduate and come back to Chiang Mai and then finally that day arrived and we were together again. We talked about our ideas for the future and she offered me the opportunity to return to live with her in America again. She told me that she had already got a good job and that it was impossible to leave her job there to move to live with me in Thailand. Throughout the time we'd been together, she had always been the giver. I had a feeling that I owed her a lot.

So, I packed my backpack again and after bidding farewell to Thailand, flew to America for the third time. It was a huge gamble for me to live abroad in order to have a better future. When the plane landed in Chicago, my girlfriend warmly welcomed me. I took a deep breath to recover from the excitement of seeing her and I promised myself that I would do my best.

We started living together again in the north of Chicago in the town of Evanston. We rented a small flat not far from the city centre and every day she went to work and I got to know the town. I applied to study English in the city, not far from our accommodation. Everything seemed to be going well for both of us. Maybe because we'd been away from each other for a long time, our relationship became stronger.

I applied for a job at a Thai restaurant called Siam Square and I was hired to work there as an assistant chef. It was my first time working in a foreign country and I had to learn and be patient when doing a job that I was not used to. I would reassure myself that things were always complicated in the beginning. The experience of working in a Thai restaurant helped me to gain knowledge and new perspectives of living in a foreign country. It made me realize that it's not as easy and comfortable as we might think. People who live abroad have to be patient and have to rely on themselves as much as possible. When I was young, I often heard that in a foreign country you can live a comfortable life, but in fact you have to work very hard for everything you get. I asked my Thai colleagues at the restaurant why they had come to work in a foreign country. The main reason was because the income was better, but many of them would have preferred a job in Thailand that paid enough to support their families. People from poor countries go to rich countries in search of a better life. They may have to leave their families behind but they do it in the hope of getting a better paid job to make their families happy.

The daily routine at the Thai restaurant of going to work at ten o'clock in the morning and finishing at midnight was monotonous. After a while I became fed up with my job and my relationship with my girlfriend began to suffer. We both worked at different times so we didn't have much time for each other. She left for work in the morning before I got up and when I came home from work she was already asleep so there was no time to talk. As time went on we grew apart. I couldn't improve my English or get used to the way of life and I felt uncomfortable living there. I became mentally weak and started to feel homesick and depressed so we had to find a solution.

After talking we concluded that it was best for us to separate for a while and have some time apart. Time would tell if and when we would be together again. If one day she or I met someone else, we would be prepared to give each other the freedom to move on. I felt bad and disappointed that I couldn't find a way to live with her and I couldn't blame anyone but myself. What would happen next? Things had changed between us so quickly and I couldn't explain why. My expectations and dreams of a comfortable life in America were but dreams after all.

I decided to pack my bags, buy a plane ticket and go back to Thailand. I carried my luggage onto the plane that day with sadness and tears as I had a foreboding feeling that this might be our last time together. Less than a week later there was the tragedy of September 11th which caused enormous damage to America. I tried to contact her to check she was safe and finally got the answer that she was fine.

No-one can predict what will happen in our lives. Humans are not made like robots with a computer system. We can't press a button to select the programme we want. We have systems that are powered by brain cells and the mind. They are complex and difficult to manage. We may try and programme our thoughts to do whatever we desire, but the results will be unpredictable. There are many things that we can't control. So don't expect too much in life, success or disappointment can appear and change our destiny at any time.

9/11 was the same whether you were a millionaire or a pauper. You could have been carrying out your daily work in a successful job with a good future. Or you might have been the homeless guy living next to a modern building like the World Trade Centre. One day, a plane crashed into that building without any warning. In the blink of an eye, it changed the fate of thousands of people in it. It was a tragedy for everybody, whether rich or poor, good or bad. They all suffered the same fate. It's the same for catastrophes such as earthquakes, storms, floods, tsunamis and even wars. There is no certainty about the life of anyone on this planet.

In Buddhism it is said that we are born with suffering. Some might argue that this is a very negative perspective, but sickness and discomfort are examples of suffering. When someone doesn't get what they desire, that is suffering. When you see or hear something that you don't like, it is a form of suffering.

Everything that exists has the potential to suffer. In fact, we are born to learn and practice how to be free from suffering. The Lord Buddha discovered and taught about the Four Noble Truths: 1) suffering, 2) the cause of suffering, 3) the end of suffering and 4) the path leading to the end of suffering. If we can work through the Four Noble Truths, we can be free from suffering.

There is a saying that like the rain or thunder, like being born or dying, if something is going to happen nobody can stop it. In this life we are just here to learn and treat anything that happens as a lesson, then let it go. If we try to cling on to things or people we love as if they belong to us, when the time comes for us to be separated, we will suffer much sadness. Buddhism teaches us to learn about and understand suffering. If we do this, we will have no suffering at all.

I never expected the simple story between me and the American girl to end with us both going our separate ways, but it happened and we just had to let it go. It was a lesson that taught me a lot about life and the future. I believe neither of us was right or wrong, there's no explanation. I felt as if someone had drawn our path and that we had arrived at a fork in that path and it was time to go our separate ways.

When things don't go as expected, you might be sad, but don't go crazy and do something stupid. Be aware of the situation and treat it as a lesson. Believe that other good things will happen in the future. In this world there is nobody who is good at everything and nobody who is bad at everything. We should live consciously and be aware of our emotions, both positive and negative, every day. If something happens, good or bad, acknowledge it and let it go. We can't always understand why things happen in this world. If at times your heart is tired from carrying so much suffering, let it go and everything will be easier.

Life is letting go!

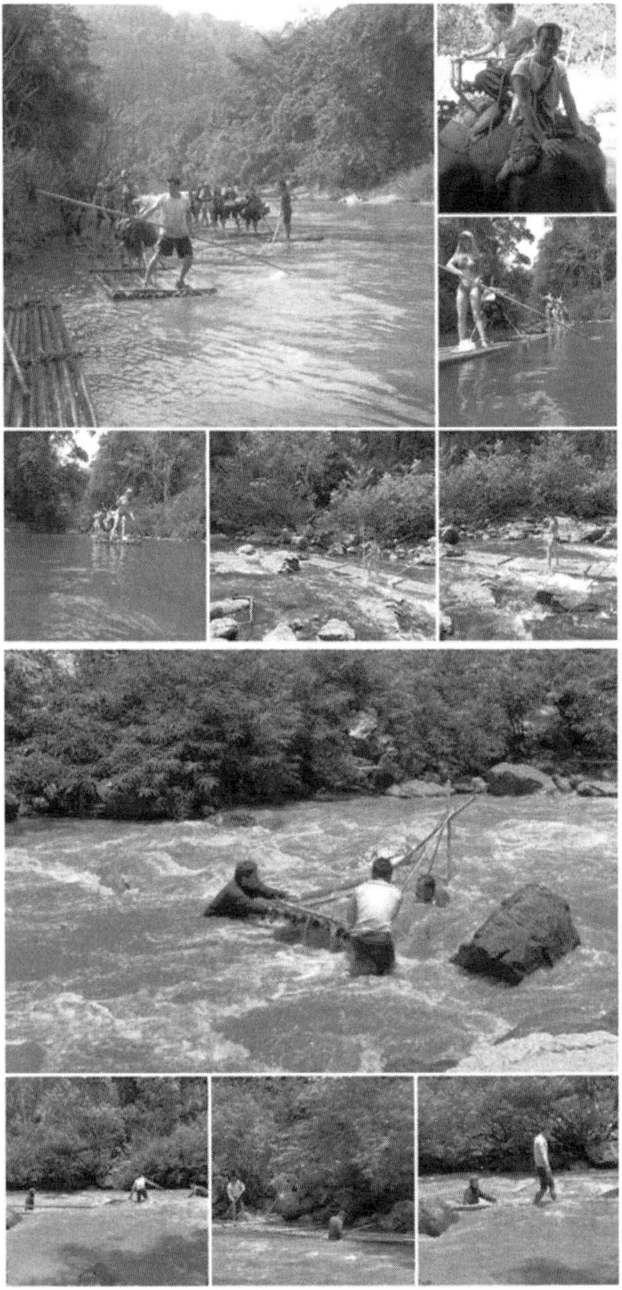

Chapter 14 - Life is Beautiful

Each person's view of and attitude towards the world varies depending on their own individual beliefs and experiences. Events throughout history have caused humanity to change. It doesn't matter when we are born, we still live in the same world. It's not the world that changes, but our minds.

After I returned from America I felt a huge disappointment in myself. The road ahead wasn't gloomy, but I felt very low. My thoughts were confused and I was overwhelmed with sadness about what had happened. The person I longed for and missed the most was my mother. It is said that where there is a mother there is a warm home.

My mother was always ready to listen to her children's troubles and to comfort and encourage. I lay in tears at her feet and told her what had happened. She stroked my head told me an old saying that people who live together who are not soulmates will one day separate. On the other hand, if you are true soulmates, no matter where you are, one day you will find each other and be together forever. Her statement was simple, but I thought I understood it well. I didn't say anything, I just nodded.

I spent time relaxing at her house in our small village in Chiang Rai province. Since leaving home to live in a temple at the age of twelve, I had never had the chance to be very close to her. It was therefore a good opportunity for me to take care of her because Buddhism teaches us to be grateful to our parents. After they raise us, we have to take care of them in return, especially when they are old.

There is a Buddhist belief that anyone born into this world without love and respect for their parents won't be successful in life and will be a selfish person. For many years, although I didn't live near my father and mother, I would try to support them by sending them money on a regular basis and making sure that they were alright.

I spent several weeks at my parents' home and it relieved my sorrow. My mother cooked the food that I liked to eat and told me stories about when I was young. It made me feel closer and more connected to her than ever.

The human mind is both good and bad, receiving messages from physical contact, the eyes, ears, nose and other parts of the body. It is something that is difficult to control and very sensitive to changing emotions of love, greed and anger. If we are not able to control our emotions, there can be serious consequences. The fact that I used to study the principles and teachings of the Buddhist way of thinking helped me to be calm and able to let go. I spent time alone, sitting and remembering various events of the past and it made me feel more positive.

Life can be beautiful depending on how well we use our mind to solve emotional problems caused by our actions. I realised that I was just selfishly clinging on to things that I didn't want to lose, which was impossible. Everything we get we will lose, if not today, then in the future. Nothing is ours permanently and nothing stays with us forever, not even our lives. When I close my eyes and reflect on past events in my life, there are many good things that I have done, both with joy and with sorrow. That is the beauty of life.

It's not important for people to be together forever. As long as we respect each other if we grow apart and remember each other with kindness, that time is not wasted. Those beautiful memories of each other will remain deep in our hearts. We can consider that we were fortunate to have spent time together in this life.

I decided to pack my bags and say goodbye to my mother and head back to Chiang Mai. I sang the 'look toong' song, a Thai country song by Khun Saengsuree Roongrot who was a popular singer when I was a child. The meaning of the song is similar to John Denver's 'Leaving on a Jet Plane', however my journey was not on a jet plane, but on an old bus. I decided it was time to continue learning and exploring this vast world to find the meaning of my life. The events that had happened in the past were valuable lessons that I had to remember. The world still had many beautiful things and challenges to explore because life is like a journey.

    Back in Chiang Mai, I went to stay with my old friend Somchai Jai-in Otto at his rented house not far from the guesthouse where he worked and I went back to my job as a trekking guide with my best friends, guide Fang and guide Manit, at Nice Place guesthouse. I worked there for a while, but got bored of doing the same route. Then one day, a friend recommended that I apply for a job as a tour leader at his company in Bangkok. When opportunities arise, we should grab them as quickly as possible so I decided to go immediately. The tour company, called Footsteps in Asia, was located in Silom Road and had its head office in Australia. There were three or four Thai employees and an Australian manager.

    On the day I applied for a job, I was confident that I would be able to work there as fortunately a lot of people I knew were already employed there. Everything seemed to go smoothly and shortly afterwards I received confirmation from the company that I could work for them as a tour leader.

    I started as a trainee, working with guide Pongsak Boonpang, a good friend of mine. I had not yet finished my training when I was called on to lead my first tour. The company saw that I had a lot of experience and they urgently needed a guide for a trip. I was very excited and grateful to be working for them. It meant that my dream had become a reality because I would have the opportunity to lead travellers to well-known tourist spots around Thailand.

    So, Footsteps in Asia was the start of a big change for me. The variety of tours on offer was very interesting and exactly what I had wanted to do for a long time. The company offered package tours, that is, tourists booked tours from abroad and my duty was to take them to the places on the itinerary. One of the rules was that we had to take our tourists to each destination by using public transport such as tuk-tuks, taxis, buses, trains and boats. We travelled like the locals so that tourists could experience their real way of life.

My first trip was the 15-day Northern Thailand & Hilltribe trek which became my favourite. I had to take tourists to Bangkok for two days, Kanchanaburi for two days, Ayutthaya, then Chiang Mai for another five days including the highlight of the trip which was a three-day two-night trek, then to Baan Tha Ton on the Myanmar border for one night, next a longtail boat ride to Chiang Rai for two days and finally Chiang Mai again to get the train back to Bangkok. It was a challenging and exciting job for me.

Through this company I experienced many things so I was very satisfied with my job. I had returned to wander on the road of tourism once again and it allowed me to quickly forget about the past because each day I was busy and had a lot of responsibilities. I travelled north and south leading tourists from all over the world to famous historical and architectural landmarks as well as the beautiful islands and beaches of Thailand. My daily life consisted of travelling with an old backpack and spending most of my time in vehicles and in hotels. My rented room was only used to store my things as I rarely had time to stay there due to travelling sometimes for months at a time.

Some of the itineraries I can remember were the 8-day Bangkok & Hilltribe Trek, 15-day Northern Thailand & Hilltribe Trek, 25-day Northern Thailand & Islands, 10-day Southern Thailand and there were many more. My life during this period was only work and I had plenty of it.

I personally don't like big cities like Bangkok and never thought about moving there because it's crowded, the traffic is crazy and it's a difficult place to live. Moreover, the way of life of the people in such big cities seems to be hurried so I felt that I wouldn't enjoy living there even though everything was so modern. Maybe it's because I had been a trekking guide for a long time, but I preferred the simple way of life in Chiang Mai, so I decided to stay there. Whenever I was assigned a tour, I took the train to Bangkok where each trip started. If you were a tour leader living in another province, the company paid your travel expenses. It suited a jungle boy like me who didn't like big cities.

When I had a tour, I would travel to Bangkok, pick up important documents from the office on Silom Road and then go to our hotel which was located in Bang Lum Phu, not far from the famous Khao San Road. The hotel, called New World Lodge, was on Sam Sen Road, Soi 2, which was quite convenient for the main tourist spots in Bangkok. After collecting all the documents, I would check them carefully to make sure there were no mistakes and that nothing was missing.

The evening was an important time when I would meet all the travellers who were booked on the trip. I introduced myself as the tour leader and gave the tourists time to get to know each other. After that I had to give them information about the journey step-by-step. The tourists came from different countries and it was quite a challenge to bring everyone together and make them feel comfortable. After this meeting I would suggest that we all go to eat and drink together in Khao San Road which was not far from the hotel. This was to give everyone the chance to become more familiar with each other before travelling together for two weeks.

Bangkok at night has many interesting things to see such as Muay Thai, the famous Thai martial art. Khao San Road is a hub for backpackers and is often the starting point for many tourists. Part of the Hollywood movie, The Beach, was filmed there making it well-known to tourists. On both sides of the road there are guesthouses, bars, live music, Thai massage, all kinds of souvenirs for sale and street food carts – it's a lively and impressive sight. Thai people who have never been there before might think that it's a city in a western country because of all the western tourists. Khao San Road never sleeps, with the sound of music coming out of each bar and crowds of people walking around, shopping, drinking, and meeting people from all over the world.

On the next day of this 15-day tour, I took the tourists sightseeing in Bangkok. We visited the Grand Palace and Wat Phra Kaew with their magnificent Thai architecture. Then we went to one of the most beautiful reclining Buddha temples in Thailand, not far from the Grand palace, Wat Pho Tha Tien. If there was still enough time left, I would offer an optional tour to take a long-tailed boat ride along the Chao Phraya river to a network of canals where you can still see the simple way of life of Bangkokians in the past.

Bangkok was founded over 200 years ago by the Chakri dynasty which still reigns today. The Chao Phraya river, which runs through it and into the Gulf of Thailand, is like a major artery that nourishes the agricultural land along the way. In the past, traders relied mainly on boats for transport as there were not many roads or vehicles. Canals were built to connect with the Chao Phraya river and every day merchants would bring their products by boats trade with each other, creating the famous floating markets.

Bangkok has been called the Venice of the East due to its many canals. Wooden raft houses float on the water and others stand on poles above it. The atmosphere is peaceful and reminiscent of a past way of life. The canals that I often took tourists to see are Khlong Bang Kruai and Khlong Mon. While taking a boat along the river, we would meet vendors on boats selling souvenirs to tourists. If one day you visit Bangkok, I definitely recommend that you do a long-tailed boat tour along the canals.

After sightseeing in Bangkok we continued our journey to Kanchanaburi. The fun started when taking tourists with their large backpacks out to catch a taxi to the southern bus terminal. It was chaos trying to find taxis for everyone. When we arrived at the bus station I had to make sure that everyone had succeeded in getting there. It was always a worry if everyone would arrive safely and on time to catch the bus to the next destination.

The local bus to Kanchanaburi took about three hours and we sat together with local passengers. Travelling like this might not be comfortable, but it gives you a real Thai experience. If you are a solo traveller, it might be a challenge to find your way to each destination but trust me it can be fun and exciting! In Kanchanaburi we stayed in a guesthouse called Jungle Floating Raft House which was a houseboat on the river Kwai. Kanchanaburi is a city of natural beauty with many tourist attractions, limestone mountains, rivers, caves and waterfalls. Unfortunately, it was also the site of some tragic events during the Second World War and the reason for our visit was to allow tourists to discover the history of the Death Railway and to see the famous bridge on the river Kwai.

During World War Two, Thailand was under the leadership of Prime Minister Phibunsongkhram. When Japanese troops invaded, the Thai government considered that it couldn't resist the Japanese army and therefore agreed to sign an alliance with them. The horror began when Japanese soldiers forced Southeast Asian civilians and allied prisoners of war to build a railway from Ban Pong in Thailand to Myanmar in order to transport troops and weapons.

The Death Railway is 415 kilometres long (303 kms in Thailand and 112 kms in Myanmar) and passes through the Three Pagodas Pass on the border between Thailand and Myanmar. Many thousands of labourers lost their lives during the construction of the railway due to horrific working conditions, starvation, disease and lack of medical equipment. It is said that every sleeper is equal to one life lost.

War, no matter when it takes place, brings cruelty and great loss to mankind. We have learned lessons from atrocities of the past, yet there are still wars going on today. It all depends on whether or not the leaders at that time are good people with good morals. Whenever we have leaders without morals, the world will not be at peace due to the selfishness of those leaders who act in their own interests regardless of the harm caused to their people. Wars often start at the hands of power-hungry leaders who won't reason or negotiate.

In Kanchanaburi I took tourists to visit important landmarks where many deaths of prisoners of war and labourers are said to have occurred. The first place is the bridge over the River Kwai, the second place is the station at Tham Krasae cave, and the third place is Hellfire pass. At Hellfire pass, there are awful stories of prisoners of war having to work all day and night. At night, they used lanterns and set up bamboo torches to provide light and while working they often heard screams of suffering as if they were in hell. Readers, if you ever visit Kanchanaburi, don't miss this place. Other places to see are the war cemetery, a cave tour and Erawan waterfall and you can also take a long-tail boat trip on the River Kwai.

We stayed there for two days and then continued our journey to the world heritage site of Ayutthaya, passing beautiful green rice fields along the way. The local passengers were excited to sit with the foreigners, but often asked me why we didn't take a more comfortable private car. I told them that tourists preferred to travel like the locals as it was more interesting.

We spent half a day visiting ancient sites and temples in the old city. Ayutthaya used to be the capital of Thailand, but it was destroyed by the Burmese army in the 18th century. In the evening, we took a sleeper train to our next destination, Chiang Mai.

Another experience that I must mention is travelling by train. During my time working as a tour leader, I had to travel from north to south by train at least ten times a month and it was like my second home. I felt safe and comfortable on the trains, because we could walk around and stretch our legs in the carriages. Train staff helped to set up tables for food and drinks so that we could socialize during the journey and when it was time to sleep, they would make up the beds. I always suggested to tourists that they buy some snacks and drinks so we could have a small party together on the train as we passed through beautiful scenery. It was a good moment to relax, talk and play games.

Sometimes we sat and ate in the dining carriage which served food and drinks until midnight and passengers from other carriages would do the same thing. There was a fun atmosphere with people from different places talking to each other and sometimes the staff would put on music for people to dance. These are memories that will stay with me forever.

The distance from Bangkok to Chiang Mai is about 700 kilometres and it takes almost 12 hours by train. Upon arrival, everything was easier for me because I felt at home there. The most exciting part of this programme was trekking in the jungle for three days and two nights. We also had time to visit Chiang Mai and in general I recommended that tourists visit Wat Phra That Doi Suthep temple, an elephant camp, the handicraft village and the Night Bazaar.

Our trek was along the Huai Nam Dang Lisu route. I had taken tourists on this route many times so there was no problem for me and my company had a big enough budget to hire several local porters to help which made everything easier for me. Being able to come back to feel the atmosphere of the jungle and mountains made me happy every time.

On this route there were various tribes living on the beautiful high mountains, elephant camps and raft camps so it was the perfect route in every way for trekking and the tourists enjoyed it. After our trek, we returned to Chiang Mai and in the evening we went to eat and drink at the Riverside pub and restaurant as I used to do.

The next day we travelled by bus to Tha Ton, a peaceful town on the border with Myanmar, to go sightseeing and stay overnight. The bus took over four hours and after checking in to our resort we walked up the mountain to see Wat Tha Ton temple and its beautiful panoramic view. The town has a large river, the Kok river, which flows from the high mountains in Myanmar into Thailand. We stayed at a small quiet resort next to the river for one night and the next day I bought tickets at the local pier for a long-tailed boat ride to Chiang Rai, which was the highlight of our trip to this town.

The Kok river is an important river that has supported the livelihoods of the locals for a long time, both for agriculture and transportation purposes. It is a charming, diverse natural river that ends at the Mekong in Chiang Rai province. This river trip has impressed and thrilled tourists for a long time thanks to its forests and mountains and farms and gardens of the villagers as well as several hilltribe villages – it's indescribably beautiful.

Some sections of the river are winding and fast with rapids so boat drivers have to be very skilled and careful. We spent almost five hours on the boat, but along the way we made regular stops to pick up and drop off passengers. The longest rest stop was at Moo Baan Karen Ruammit village, which is right next to the water's edge. It is a large area that includes many tribes living together where tourists can do elephant trekking and buy local products from the market.

Finally, we arrived at the Mae Fah Luang Bridge in Chiang Rai, tired from travelling all day, and I contacted the minibus service to take us to the hotel where we would stay while we visited the city for two days and two nights.

Chiang Rai is an old city that was built by King Mengrai and has many ancient buildings such as temples and pagodas as well as art and culture. It was a prosperous city in the early days of the Mengrai dynasty, but later the king made Chiang Mai the new capital of the Lanna Kingdom.

We visited Wat Rong Khun - the white temple, Tham Pla cave, crossed the border to visit Tha Khe Lek town in Myanmar, then visited the Hall of Opium Museum in Chiang Saen and the Chedi Luang temple viewpoint area at the Golden Triangle where Thailand, Myanmar and Laos meet at The Mekong river. Finally, we travelled back to Chiang Mai where we caught the train back to Bangkok.

As a tour guide, I led travellers on journeys north and south, to islands in the Gulf of Thailand; Koh Samui, Koh Pha Ngan and Koh Tao, and also in the Andaman Sea; Phuket, Krabi, Phang Nga and Trang. I got paid to go to places that people dream of visiting, it was a career that brought me a lot of happiness. Happiness depends on the individual, just follow your heart and be happy with the things that you've done. Live consciously in the present, accept what happens and don't get attached to either good or bad emotions. The essence of existence is that we can let go of our ego and suffer less.

A year after returning from America and working for this new company, destiny drew a new path for me. No one knows what will happen to them in the future. Our lives are dynamic, leading to changes all the time, we can only do our best for today.

The next tour I led was an eight-day Bangkok and hilltribe trek. On this programme we started in Bangkok then travelled to Northern Thailand for a four-day three-night trek in Chiang Mai. I travelled from Chiang Mai to Bangkok to pick up my clients as usual. There were six of them; five Australians and one British woman. After introductions we went to eat together at Khao San Road. Everything went smoothly because it was a small group. The next day we visited Bangkok and in the evening we took the night train to Chiang Mai. While on the train we had a small party – it was fun and I felt quite comfortable with everyone.

The Trekking Guide   ชีวิตข้าไกด์ทัวร์ป่า

We visited Wat Phra That Doi Suthep, Mae Sa Elephant Camp and then Bo Sang Umbrella Craft Centre for a half-day sightseeing tour and in the evening I organised a meeting to prepare for the trek – everyone seemed excited about it. On this route we would travel to Lisu Huai Nam Dang over four days. I hired two porters to help me, Gaga and Somdee, Karen hilltribe people whose village we stayed at on the second day.

The next day after breakfast we headed by minibus to Mae Taeng district on the way to Huai Nam Dang national park, stopping at Mae Malai market to buy food for the trip. We picked up my two porters along the way and visited beautiful waterfalls around Baan Mae Sae village.

When the minibus dropped us off, we picked up our backpacks and started hiking into the mountains and through beautiful scenery to reach Moo Baan Lisu Huai Nam before dusk. It took almost three and a half hours. That evening Gaga and Somdee lit a fire to boil water for tea and coffee and to cook dinner for the travellers. During October the weather high on the mountains in Northern Thailand is cold so we built a campfire to keep warm. After dinner, we talked about our day and drank Lisu corn liquor to keep away the cold - it was a simple but very special night for me.

On the second day, we stayed overnight at Gaga and Somdee's village, Mae Jok Karen village. The two young men volunteered to lead us on this route as they had grown up in the area and knew it well. Although I had taken tourists on the Huai Nam Dang route many times, I had never passed this way before. We trekked through beautiful green forest with small waterfalls and various types of plants. The tourists were impressed with the natural beauty of the area.

After walking for a while we came across rice fields and herds of water buffaloes and there were bamboo huts belonging to villagers that were perfect for a lunchbreak. We made lunch, had a rest and then carried on hiking until we reached Moo Baan Mae Jok at about five o'clock.

This village was located on a high mountain overlooking forests and terraced rice fields. There were about thirty families living a simple life there like that of their ancestors, without cars or electricity, growing crops and raising animals. The travellers got up early to take pictures and after breakfast we packed our bags and continued our journey. We walked to Karen Pa Khao Lam village for lunch and then to Plang Pakha elephant camp next to the Mae Taeng river where the tourists rode elephants to a Lahu village, Moo Baan Pong Ngan Lahu, for the third night.

This Lahu village was located near the banks of the river and was home to about twenty families. It was the village where tourists from various trekking companies all went to stay overnight because it was located at a point where it took just the right amount of time to reach the next village by bamboo raft. In the evening, we had fun bathing in the river with the village children, then the porters and I cooked dinner. It was our last night in the jungle together and after dinner we had a drink - it was a wonderful night.

The next day we travelled by bamboo raft for about three hours to Moo Baan Sob Kai village and returned to Chiang Mai by minibus. In the evening, we celebrated at the Riverside restaurant and the next day we took the train back to Bangkok. Everything had gone smoothly and the tourists had got along well together.

It is impossible to know who decides our destiny. If the day comes when we meet someone and become a couple, it will happen without us expecting it. It was like my mother had told me, if people are soulmates, regardless of where they are one day they will meet. During this trip I met my future wife.

Over the week that I was leading the trip, the British woman and I had got to know each other and we got along well. After the trip I showed her around Bangkok for a few more days before she travelled to Australia. On the day we had to say goodbye, we didn't know what would happen in the future. We both felt sad and all I could do in that moment was wish her luck and a safe trip and hope that we would meet again. We exchanged phone numbers and email addresses and promised that we would keep in touch.

A few months later I received the good news from her that she was coming back to Thailand. After returning home to England she had decided to look for a job at an English language school in Chiang

Mai. Soon after, she arrived and we became a couple and the story of my life with my wife began.

When she became pregnant I was afraid and happy at the same time because I didn't expect that something like this could happen to me. I was a little concerned that I wouldn't be up to the job, but also so pleased that I would be a father - wow! Life is hard to predict - whether it's decided by God or whoever I don't know, but in any case we stayed together.

We agreed that she would give birth in England and I would travel to join her. In October 2003, we welcomed our son, Benjapon, meaning a boy who has five strengths. I was indescribably proud. We went to the Thai embassy in London to apply for Thai citizenship for him and at the same time we registered our marriage – we were now husband and wife.

Everybody's life story is uncertain – don't expect any certainty. Do you believe in fate, destiny, merit and karma or not? Some people may believe that life depends on our actions, that we determine our own destiny. True, our lives do depend on our actions - we may have a plan or a goal that we would like to achieve – but the outcome is unpredictable. Perhaps it's in the hands of someone we call God?

Over the past years I have pondered and searched for answers to the events that have happened in my life. I am surprised by things which have happened to me as a poor trekking guide, which in many ways seemed improbable. I wonder what my life would be like if I hadn't left America. It's a question that can't be answered and it's pointless to think about what might have been.

I am proud of myself for having the opportunity to write this book and to have a son and a warm family. I can't say that everything that happens is decided by God. However to me,

Life is beautiful!

Yao Sripuri

Chapter 15 - Life is a Nature Lesson

What is the most important thing in life? It's a question to which I don't seek an answer because each person's response is probably different. We can't judge whether the things other people consider important in their lives are right or wrong. The thoughts and desires of each individual are difficult to explain to others and so one person's answer may not be the same as another's.

I myself am an optimistic person who doesn't get too attached to the various things that happen in life, but I still feel love, greed, anger and delusion like any other human. When these feelings arise, it's difficult to control them and not make mistakes. However, I try to use Buddha's teachings to remind me to think positively, do good deeds and remain in the present moment as much as possible.

After our son was born, we stayed in England until he was three months old then we went back to Thailand. I had previously opened a trekking company in Chiang Mai and I had to go back to run the tours. We rented a small house near Chiang Mai Gate in Baan Suan Kiethavee village next to an area called Kad Kom. It had two bedrooms, a living room, bathroom and kitchen and was sufficient for a small family. At that time, I had many friends who were also married to foreign women living in Chiang Mai so we weren't lonely.

I returned to running my trekking business and a friend and I explored a route in Wiang Pa Pao district, near my village. I chose this route because I wanted to show tourists how to survive in the jungle and learn about the way of life of the hilltribes. With my customers we explored nature without elephant riding or bamboo rafting. As the aim was to travel in an eco-friendly way, I only took a maximum of six people at a time.

This trek took three days and two nights along an unexplored and challenging route for adventurous travellers. On the first day we walked for three hours and on the second day we walked for seven to eight hours. My first customers were a German couple named Marcus and Eva. On day one we travelled north by public bus to Wiang Pa Pao, with a short stop at a local market before continuing to my parents' house for lunch. After that we walked through beautiful mountains to a remote Karen village which had never been visited by tourists. We stayed with P'Ai's (Mr Ai's) family, spending time learning from them while intruding as little as possible on the local way of life.

On day two, P'Ai offered to guide us to another village and teach us how to live in the forest. We hiked through beautiful scenery and dense jungle for almost four hours, passing through a Lahu village where the locals gathered round to see westerners for the first time. Marcus, who was a doctor in Germany, helped some of the children who were unwell.

We continued our journey, stopping at a waterfall to cool off and learn jungle cooking and survival skills with P'Ai. Everyone was tired, but the amazing views kept us going. Finally, we reached a small Lahu village which had no more than four or five houses high on a mountain. We had walked for a total of seven hours that day.

On day three, we said goodbye to P'Ai who returned to his village having received a tip from Marcus and Eva who were so grateful for his help. Then we trekked for three to four hours up and down mountains to another Lahu village, the last one on the border between Chiang Rai and Chiang Mai. We stopped for lunch there and paid a villager who owned a pick-up truck to drive us back to Chiang Mai. My customers were very impressed with their trip and promised to recommend me and send me other customers.

However, although we did get more customers, it was not enough to cover our costs and unfortunately, I had to shut down my trekking company after less than two years. I was disappointed that I couldn't make enough money from the business that I had put my heart into and I was left with almost no income.

At that point, my wife decided to go back to teaching again and leave the responsibility of taking care of our son to me which I did until he was two years old and started Nandachart Kindergarten in Chiang Mai. I then had time to earn some money by leading treks for local companies, but even so I was worried about how I could earn enough money to support my family. In the end I decided to return to work as a tour leader in Bangkok as I had done before. Some friends I used to work with suggested I apply for a job at the company where they were working, ETC, which stood for Education Travel Centre. It was a large firm located on Ratchadamnoen Road, not far from Khao San Road. It was well-known and trusted by foreign companies who sent their customers there. It wasn't long before I heard that I had been accepted and started working for ETC.

Backpacking was a popular way of travelling and tourists liked to go with local guides for simplicity and to be able to access local areas more easily. Some people didn't want to organize travel themselves because it could be difficult. Therefore, trips like this were fully booked every month and we guides were so busy that we rarely had time for a holiday.

I had returned to work as a tour guide again, but now I had a family to take care of and I didn't have the same freedom as before. It was difficult for those of us with families because we were often away for almost a month. It was easier for single people to do this type of work as they didn't have anyone else to consider.

After a while I began to see many problems and obstacles. It was difficult - I still liked working as a trekking guide, but at the same time having a family brought many responsibilities. I knew that one day I would have to do something different in order to support my family. My wife and I had some disagreements about the work I was doing, but there was not much choice for me who had been a trekking guide for most of my life.

As trekking was one of the most popular activities at the time, ETC started to work with a local trekking company in Chiang Mai, Udomporn Tours, to explore a new three-day two-night trip along the Muang Khong - Sob Kai route. The idea was to use a local trekking guide in addition to the tour leader. In my opinion, the policy of using local guides to work with tour leaders was a good thing because it helped to provide an income to local people.

One day I was assigned to do the 15-day Northern Thailand and Hilltribe Trek, which included the new Chiang Mai trekking route. I had a trainee guide with me who was a friend I had recommended to ETC as they needed a lot of tour guides at that time. Together we took our tourists around Bangkok, Kanchanaburi, and Ayutthaya and then to Chiang Mai. I was excited to explore this new route and I contacted a local trekking guide to plan the trip.

I was happy to be able to go back to the area again. Muang Khong is a village in Chiang Dao district. In the past, this charming village in the mountains had not had much contact with outsiders due to its remoteness and inaccessibility. The road was a narrow dirt track with steep forested areas on both sides. There were also various ethnic hilltribe villages - Karen, Lisu, Lahu, Hmong and Akha - scattered high in the mountains, blending perfectly with nature.

Once trekking guides had taken tourists to this area, its natural beauty was revealed and so other tour companies started to go there in order to explore routes for more adventurous travellers. This led to demand from travellers to go and experience the beauty of nature and the simple way of life of the people who lived there and the village became well-known for trekking. As more foreigners started to pass through, it gave the villagers the opportunity to practice speaking other languages and communicate with tourists.

I had some fun times on that route. For this trip I had the trainee guide, twelve tourists who were Australian, American, English, Irish and German and our local trekking guide, Susin, who was a young Karen man with excellent knowledge of the jungle. His assistant was a porter called Phi Nan Kan. 'Phi Nan' is a term that honours people who have been ordained and educated in the temple. My name is Yao and I was ordained as a monk, so people call me 'Phi Nan Yao'.

When I asked Phi Nan Kan why he had left the monkhood, he replied that he wanted to work and earn money in order to support his parents. He told me that he wanted to improve his English and that he hoped to work as a trekking guide in the future so I decided that if tourists had questions during the trek, I would tell them to ask him so that he could practice his English as much as possible. He reminded me of myself when I was just starting out and I wished him success.

On the first day of the trek, we set off for Muang Kong village in two cars. As usual, we stopped at a market on the way to get some provisions for three days and two nights in the jungle, then we continued our journey into Doi Chiang Dao National Park. We had lunch at a viewpoint high up in the park where you could see tall mountains interspersed with white clouds floating in front of your eyes, it was beautiful. When we arrived at Muang Khong village we said goodbye to the driver who we would see again in three days' time at Sob Kai village.

Susin told everyone to pick up their backpacks and we started walking into the jungle towards Huai Din Dam Lisu village. He told us that today would be an easy day, taking about two hours to reach our destination. The weather in Thailand is around 35-40 degrees every day, making it difficult for European tourists who are not used to it, but as we walked through the forest and farmland we cooled down a bit.

Sometimes we took breaks to recover and answer travellers' questions about what they had seen. On that day, an Australian man named Rodney had noticed a dead tree that looked like it had been burned by fire. He was surprised and asked the porter, Nan Kan, what had happened to the tree. The porter tried to explain - I didn't hear what he said but I could see that Rodney looked confused.

We arrived at the village of Lisu Huai Din Dam that evening and after dinner we sat and chatted and drank together. I told the tourists about the history of the village and the way of life of the Lisu people. Rodney mentioned the dead tree he had seen. He said that the porter had said "That tree is for the tea for the coffee for you!".

When I asked the porter what he had said to Rodney, he said he'd explained that the tree was dead and that he would use it to make a fire to boil water for tea and coffee for him. I told Rodney that the tree had probably been struck by lightning which caused it to burn and die, but Nan Kan meant that he would bring it to use as firewood to boil water for tea and coffee. The misunderstanding became a joke that we laughed about all evening!

That night we built a fire and danced with the villagers and children. This is a traditional Lisu way of welcoming and showing respect to visitors. The elderly Lisu men played traditional musical instruments and held hands as they danced in a circle around the fire. We all enjoyed the dances and were amused by the unfamiliar Lisu traditions. Whenever I went trekking I was always happy to see the smiles on the faces of tourists and villagers and it made me proud of my work.

The next day, villagers brought souvenirs they had made by hand to sell to tourists - the Lisu people are skilled in embroidery - and I encouraged the group to help support the local community by buying some items. Once everyone had packed their backpacks, we thanked the host in Lisu, "Akupumu", and left Huai Din Dam village via the villagers' farms towards the high mountains above. We passed some graves which the tourists were curious about and I explained that according to Lisu tradition, when someone dies, the village shaman chooses a place and throws an egg in the air. Where it lands is where the grave is dug and surrounded by a bamboo fence.

The local guide, Susin, warned everyone that the journey would be quite difficult that day because we had to climb several hills and cross a river and as we walked through the forest along the villagers' path it seemed that the mountains would never end. We continued up and down hills until we reached the Mae Taeng River where we had to cross to the other side. The locals had tied a large rope from one side to the other attached to trees. We had to hold on to the rope with our hands while carefully crossing the river. We advised everyone to take off their shoes first because if they got wet, they would be heavy, making it more difficult. We helped each other across and eventually everyone made it safely to the other side.

We carried on until we reached an elephant camp in the late afternoon. Everyone was obviously tired from trekking by then so we advised the tourists to take a refreshing swim in the river and relax while waiting for lunch. When the mahouts brought the elephants to bathe, the tourists were excited to see them up close and to be able to play with them in the water. We had noodle soup for lunch, then the tourists rode elephants to Karen Pa Khao Lam village where we spent the second night. Everything had gone according to plan and we arrived at the village before nightfall, exactly as we had anticipated.

Karen Pa Khao Lam is a large village located next to the river with a school for children from the area. In the evenings, the men, women and children of the village, and also cows and buffaloes, all went down to wash and play in the river. It was beautiful to see, this simple way of life of people who lived in the forest.

When we arrived there, Susin contacted a family who agreed to let us stay at their house. I told the travellers to get changed and go to bathe in the river with the villagers. That evening, it was a strange sight to see foreign tourists in bikinis swimming alongside the giggling local children!

I had stayed there many times so I knew the villagers quite well. Some of them who liked to drink would come and join me if they found out I was staying there, so I invited the tourists to help cook and drink together with them. The small kitchen was full of fun and laughter with both foreigners and villagers sitting in a circle happily sharing moonshine and beer.

While cooking, a German woman asked the porter Nan Kan "What are you cooking for us tonight?". He cheerfully replied "Fuk soup". The tourists were shocked and looked at each other in confusion. I had to apologize and explain that the porter wasn't swearing. 'Fuk' is Thai for 'pumpkin' - we were having pumpkin soup! Everyone laughed loudly and said "Okay, let's eat fuk soup this evening!".

After dinner we went outside to make a bonfire and the children of the village came along to sing songs with us. There were a lot of children in the village and one of the tourists asked why there were so many. So, I told a story that may or may not be based on true events!

Many years ago, some remote villages didn't have access to public health services and the population increased rapidly because the villagers didn't understand birth control. The government set up a programme to teach villagers about contraception and one of the ministers named Meechai started a stall selling vegetables, clothes and condoms which was called Cabbages and Condoms. Then he opened a small restaurant which has become quite a well-known chain. Its motto at that time was that the food was guaranteed not to cause pregnancy.

The story goes that when health officials took condoms to the villagers, they demonstrated how to use them by putting them on their thumbs and explained that they were a magic way of preventing their wives from getting pregnant. It later emerged that village men had been naively putting condoms on their thumbs as advised by the health officials which explained why hilltribe people continued to have many children!

Soon, it was the last night of our trek through hilltribe villages. Although it wasn't anything like as comfortable as a hotel, all the tourists seemed to be happy and enjoying themselves. We played games with the kids and sang together. The trainee guide played the guitar and sang very well, attracting the attention of the western girls. It was a wonderful and memorable time for all of us and the porter, Nan Kan, was able to chat and practice English in a friendly environment. When we asked him if he could speak English, he said no but he could speak 'Thailish' (Thai-English) haha!

The next morning, we woke up with hangovers and fuelled up with a big breakfast before setting off on a bamboo rafting trip to Sob Kai Village. It's a journey that takes about four hours if all goes well. The evening before, the local guide Susin had asked some villagers to build two rafts which could each carry eight people and when everything was ready, we thanked our host and the villagers in the Karen language, "Ta Bu". I steered one of the rafts and Susin took the other. I had a lot of experience of rafting down the Mae Taeng river and I always joked that if the tourists wanted to be safe, they should travel on my raft as I had a bamboo raft driving licence!

After two hours we stopped at Lahu Pong Ngan village for a rest and to allow the tourists to have a look around the village, then we continued along the river. This part could take two to three hours depending on the situation because there were rapids and we had to be careful not to have any accidents. We managed to get through the more dangerous part and safely arrived at Sob Kai village where we had lunch and were picked up by car to go back to our hotel in Chiang Mai.

The tourists were grateful for our teamwork which had made the trip so special and full of smiles and laughter and gave tips to Susin and Nan Kan. The trainee guide and I continued with them the next day to the border town of Tha Ton and Chiang Rai. A few days later we spent our last evening together on the train from Chiang Mai to Bangkok. We bought some beer to celebrate and talked about our time travelling together over the past fifteen days. Everyone agreed that it had been amazing. We then went to the 'disco' in the dining carriage and stayed until it was closed before going to our beds to sleep until we arrived in Bangkok in the early morning.

Thanks to my time working as a tour leader for ETC, taking groups from Bangkok to the north and south of Thailand, I have enough experience to suggest places to visit if you get the chance to go to Thailand. I recommend Northern Thailand with a hilltribe trek and also Khao Sok National Park, which is one of the few remaining rainforests in the south of Thailand. This area of natural beauty has an abundance of animals, birds, insects and plants and is definitely worth a visit. Not to be missed is an overnight stay in a houseboat at Ratchaprapha Dam. The dam was built to generate electricity and provide water to Phang Nga and Krabi provinces and with its tall limestone mountains, the view is so beautiful it looks like a Chinese painting.

In this area there are plenty of things to do for nature lovers such as long-tail boat trips, swimming, canoeing and kayaking, watching hornbills, nighttime wildlife spotting and visiting caves and waterfalls. To get there from Bangkok you can take a train to Surat Thani then book a bus from a local travel agency nearby.

In Southern Thailand there are many beautiful islands and beaches such as Koh Samui, Koh Phangan, Koh Tao, Phuket, Krabi and Koh Phi Phi. I also recommend Koh Mook in Trang province, which is a place that sticks in my memory. This small island where villagers make their living by fishing and on rubber plantations is not as busy as Phuket and Krabi. It has lots of beaches, each with their own underwater world filled with shoals of fish and coral. If you want peace and privacy, Koh Mook is like paradise with its clear emerald green water. You can camp on the beach and go snorkelling and fishing and it also has a cave that you can swim into. The Koh Mook Rubber Tree Resort is a quiet little resort about five hundred metres from the beach. The owner, Mr Nutthapong Maknakorn, is kind and welcomes you like a friend. You can contact him directly to get there and he will take care of everything you need.

My choice to live as a trekking guide changed many things for me. I learned a lot and met many people. It might be an insignificant life story for some, but for me it has been great. What was troublesome in this job, however, was my love of drinking alcohol. No matter where I went, there was always an opportunity to sit and drink with new friends. I don't remember when I started drinking, probably when I began working as a trekking guide, and it has been a habit ever since.

When I reflect on my childhood, I remember the bad behaviour of my father when he was drunk. I used to scold him and I made a promise to myself that I would not drink and ruin my reputation or do harm to my family. In fact, I'm not an alcoholic who needs to drink all the time, I just enjoy hanging out and drinking with friends.

However, liquor, drugs and all intoxicating substances ultimately do more harm than good – they affect our health and cause us to lose money. Sometimes when we stray into habits such as drinking and taking drugs, it's hard to find a way out. In Buddhism it is said there is no one who can help us but ourselves. It all depends on how smart we are to be able to correct our own mistakes.

My wife and I agreed that when our son turned four we would move to England for his education. My life as a trekking guide began to come to an end in 2007. Our role in life is always changing depending on the various situations that we encounter. Of course, our lives are our own and we can choose our direction and goals, can't we? That's true if we are single – we have the freedom to choose. But if we have a partner by our side, there are other factors to consider. It's not always easy for two people who live together to agree because they each have their own ideas. If both sides' thinking and goals match, then it is a good thing and they can move forwards together towards a common destination. If they don't, they must find a way to reach a compromise, However, if both sides stand firm in their own opinions without accepting each other's good and bad points, there will be only conflict. Marriage can be a fragile thing that requires reasoning, patience and mutual respect.

I was getting tired of the tour guide lifestyle which meant I had to be away from my family and I missed the comfort of being together. I saw that I had to make a change in order to take care of my family. For a long time, I was stuck in my comfort zone and enjoying myself, but now I had two other people to think about. This world was still beautiful and there were still so many things to explore. I would keep the memories and experiences of the past years deep in my heart so I would not forget them.

Everything that has a beginning has an end. Our lives are like dramas that follow a storyline, but we are not sure who the writer is. Have you ever asked yourself why you were born? If we still don't know, or are unsure of our answer, then we should not be angry about the way other people live their lives because sometimes we don't even understand our own thoughts or actions. We can't criticise people if we ourselves are not perfect. Let time and the law of karma be the judge.

Many people may say that they want to have a good life, but what is a good life? If it means being physically comfortable and financially free, but without the love and warmth of a family, it might be meaningless. In my opinion, a good life comes from a warm family with love, understanding and forgiveness. It is not necessary to be jealous of the life of a rich family. It is not certain that all is as it seems and it may not be a good life.

Let's go back to the question I asked in the first line of this chapter. What is the most important thing in life? It's a fact of life that when we are born, we have to die. Death is something that we fear because it's difficult for us to understand where we go. In

Buddhism, those who have achieved enlightenment have learnt and understood the Four Noble Truths and are not afraid of death because they know where they will go next.

It is said that a person will only know the truth about life when he is on his deathbed. The most valuable and meaningful thing at that moment is the breath. Once a body has lost its breath, everything in this world is no longer important or meaningful. Life without breath is like a piece of wood. So, when we are still alive, breath and good health are the most important things in life.

The Dalai Lama has said that humans are the strangest things in the world. We sacrifice our health to make money and then we sacrifice money to get our health back. We are so worried about the future that we are unhappy with the present, as a result we are absent from both the present and the future. We live as if we will never die, and in the end, we die without having lived.

I would like to ask you, dear readers, from the moment you were born, what have you given to the world? How much love, understanding and compassion have you shared with those who live in the world with you? How much have you tried to reduce your feelings of greed, anger and hatred? What can you give to this world? Lord Budha said that the easiest thing to give, if we have nothing else, is forgiveness. The gifts of love, kindness and forgiveness are very valuable. If we can give these, then we can be released from negative emotions and, when the time comes for us to go, we can leave this world peacefully.

In March 2008, my wife, son and I left Thailand and travelled to England to start a new life. Goodbye forests, mountains and streams. I have left a footprint in every hilltribe village that I have visited. All the stories of joy and sorrow that I experienced and the life lessons I learned as a trekking guide will be etched in my memory for the rest of my life.

Life is a nature lesson!

Conclusion

No matter what kind of work you choose to do to support yourself and your family, give yourself hope and encouragement first, and then proceed with that mission to the best of your ability.

Don't let fear stop you. The fear of failure will keep you from reaching your goal of success. The fear of losing keeps us from trying to win. When we are afraid to let go of people or things, we will never be able to walk or swim to the other side.

The value of being born as a human being is not measured by wealth, but by being a good person and having compassion for those who are less fortunate. Let's use this remaining life of ours to benefit ourselves and others. Just by doing this, our lives will not be in vain.

A few years ago, on one of my trips back to Thailand, I had the opportunity to go on a trek on the Mae Taeng river route, but this time I went as a tourist. It made me very happy to see old places and do things that I had often done in the past. I met many young generation trekking guides who used to be my porters, but who had now themselves become trekking guides.

In a quiet corner of a hilltribe village by the river, I closed my eyes and with a smile of happiness thought to myself:

"I am a trekking guide".

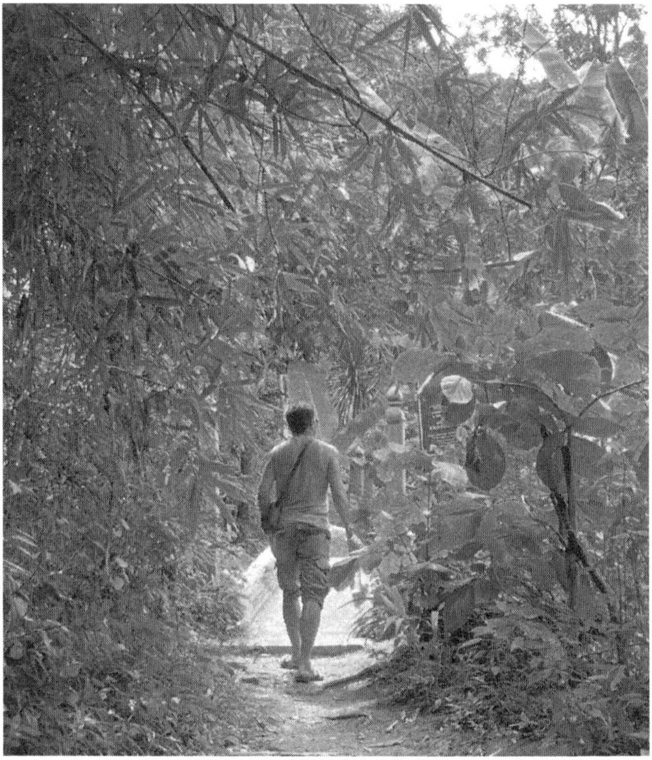

Punsawat Sripuri (Yao) was born on 22nd December 1970 in a small village named San Nong Bua, Chiang Rai province, Thailand. At the age of 12 he went to live in a temple and was ordained as a novice monk in 1984. He left the monkhood to work as a tour guide from 1992 until 2008. He is married and has a son and currently lives in the south west of England.

Printed in Great Britain
by Amazon